EASTBOUR BUS STORY

Dave Spencer

Cover photographs -

Top - Passing along the seafront is No 96. New to Eastbourne Corporation in 1936, it was converted to an open topper in 1956 and was known as the "White Knight".

Bottom - Southdown No 412 is heading up Terminus Road passing the remains of the Gildredge Hotel. The bus was a wartime utility model on a Guy Arab chassis with Park Royal bodywork. Converted to open top in 1951, it received a Weymann body in 1958. Just one instance of the detail which makes vehicle histories so fascinating.

 Middleton Press

*To Mandy for putting up with the mess and
John for his encouragement.*

8th April 1993

As I am in the position, by chance, to be managing the successor company to the World's first

municipal motor bus undertaking in it's 90th year, it gives me pleasure to welcome

this interesting publication on Eastbourne's buses.

D R Howard,
Managing Director.

First Published June 1993

ISBN 1 873793 17 0

© Copyright D. Spencer 1993

Design - Deborah Goodridge

*Published by Middleton Press
        Easebourne Lane
        Midhurst, West Sussex
        GU29 9AZ
        Tel: (0730) 813169
(From April 1995 (01730) 813169)*

*Printed and bound by Biddles Ltd,
        Guildford and Kings Lynn*

CONTENTS

MAPS

Nominal route numbers for Corporation services as in 1936. Brewery advertising in the Corporation timetables in the 1930's accounted for most advertising revenue, although most of the public houses mentioned required a substantial walk from the nearest town bus service.

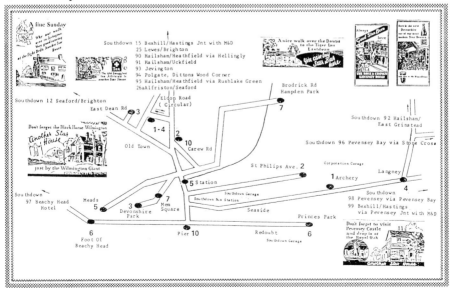

INTRODUCTION

This volume has been published to coincide with the 90th anniversary of municipal transport in Eastbourne. The borough was the first authorised to run motor buses in the world, the earliest vehicles predating number plates and like their horse drawn competition carried police licence badges. Horse buses soon vanished from the avenues of Edwardian Eastbourne, just as the stagecoach had already succumbed to the railway in the 19th century. Wagonettes and charabancs ran day trippers to Beachy Head whilst donkeys, goats and dogs provided the motive power for rides along the seafront.

Transport in East Sussex was hampered by some of the worst roads in the Kingdom although by the first world war Worthing Motor Services and their successors, Southdown Motor Services, had extended coastal services eastward to Eastbourne. Southdown and Eastbourne Corporation agreed running powers within the borough boundaries and little competition took place for decades.

Recovery from the gloom of the great war saw the expansion of excursions and tours, former horse bus operator, Chapmans, provided the largest independent coach business in the town. Their pristine primrose coloured saloons laid the foundations for Southdown's renowned tours. The Corporation were innovative in their body building activities, their workshops producing one of the country's first covered top double deck buses. As the century progressed, bus travel was increasingly within the grasp of the working man. Bus services expanded to the new estates and by the thirties a basic pattern of services existed which would last forty years.

Those heady inter-war years in Eastbourne were exemplified by the municipal bus fleet, each vehicle turned out gleaming with paintwork finished off in gold lining. Similar standards were maintained by Southdown Motor Services with whom one could journey to the pleasures of Wannock Tea Gardens or quaint villages such as Pevensey or Alfriston.

The Second World War had inevitable consequences for the town and its bus fleets. Being on the front line, the seafront became a restricted area. With much of the population evacuated and deprived of visitors, the surplus buses assisted the war effort as far away as Lancashire. The numerous air raids on the town included direct hits on buses and widespread damage at the railway station. Phoenix like the buses which lay mangled at the hands of the Luftwaffe emerged again with new bodies. As post war supplies trickled through, the more elderly pre-war buses and in the case of Southdown those built to spartan wartime standards were given a new lease of life as open toppers. A boom in holidays offset the gloom of austerity, as did a series of hot summers.

Eastbourne was indeed the "suntrap of the South" but this was an Indian summer for bus operators. Car ownership, holidays abroad and escalating running costs contributed to a story of decline as passengers turned away from public transport. In the 1980s many initiatives were tried in an effort to stem the decline; the use of mini buses brought services to roads previously unserved. Changes in legislation took operators in to new areas beyond their former boundaries. As you will see through the following pages, many features of Eastbourne's buses do remain to the delight of transport enthusiasts and visitors alike. Visitors still ride on open top buses to Beachy Head and coaches pick up outside the restored pier entrance; new developments such as the marina and an extended season may call for increased services. The regular influx of foreign students and the resurgence of British holidays already makes heavy demands upon the operators in the peak season. Although only a snapshot of just some vehicles, characters and routes, I hope that you will find this a fitting tribute to ninety years of municipal buses in Eastbourne and, in an age of enlightened attitudes towards our environment, make full use of the present services.

Dave Spencer
Lower Peover, Cheshire. August 1992.

PUBLISHER'S NOTE

Deep gratitude is expressed to Mr D.R.Howard, Managing Director of Eastbourne Buses Ltd., for checking the text for factual accuracy and for ensuring that nothing is published that could cause offence in the delicate subject of competition.

1. THE EARLY YEARS

Bumpy roads and a shakey start

The impetus for the expansion from hackney carriages to horsed omnibuses arrived in the shape of the London Brighton and South Coast Railway which opened its branch service to Eastbourne on May 14th 1849. With due ceremony to the strains of a brass band a fifteen hour programme of celebrations which included fireworks and acrobats heralded in a new era for transport to Eastbourne. The ordinary working man saw what was probably his first locomotive and perhaps took the opportunity to take a short ride in an open truck.

The LBSCR had opened its Brighton to Hastings line in 1846 and provided a station at Polegate for Eastbourne passengers.

The enterprising landlord of the Anchor and Sea House Hotel Mr D. Burford, operated some sort of omnibus between Polegate and his hostelery at Seahouses. This service connected with the Lewes train and lasted until the Eastbourne branch was opened. Travel to the coast was quite expensive but soon proved more than a match for the stage coach service.

The collection of hamlets which formed East Bourne were brought to national attention by illustrious visitors such as the children of George III. Their stay at the Round House must have caused quite a stir as just a few years before the seaside was considered very unhealthy. The Prince Regent developed nearby Brighthelmstone into the flamboyant and fashionable resort of Brighton, whilst in Eastbourne carefully planned developments were guided by the Duke of Devonshire. Travelling facilities to Eastbourne in the late eighteenth century were thought to be remarkably good considering that East Sussex had remained a backwater whilst the industrial revolution swept the country. In 1795 a stagecoach left for London over some of the worst roads in the kingdom. In the capital it stopped at the Elephant & Castle and Charing Cross where it arrived at 5.30pm. It left Charing Cross every morning except Sunday at 8am bound for Seahouses.

The next date for which we have any great detail is about 1830. Reed's van provided a scheduled goods and passenger service which departed for Brighton and Lewes from the Star Inn every Monday, Wednesday and Friday at 1pm. It called on its return to Hastings at 2pm on Tuesday, Thursday and Saturdays. Heavier loads together with passengers went to Lewes and London by carriers such as James Hoad, John Jarrett, Zebedee Davis and Isaac Leney. The prestige services however were the fast stage coaches (the intercity service of its day) which also carried post and were named to reflect the virtues of the service offered.

From William Boy's New Inn in South Street every Monday, Wednesday and Friday at 9am the "Safety" coach left for London via Hailsham, Horsebridge, East Hoathly,

LIVERY STABLES AND FLY PROPRIETORS.

CLIFTON MEWS,

◄ LIVERY AND BAIT STABLES, ►

SOUTH STREET, EASTBOURNE.

Rear of Clifton Hotel and near St. Saviour's Church.

OPEN AND

CLOSE

CARRIAGES.

PONY-CHAISE,

&c., LET

ON HIRE.

The arrangements are most complete, each Stable being divided into Stalls and Loose Boxes, with Coach-house and Harness-room, and Coachman's and Groom's furnished apartments adjoining. All fitted with every convenience.

R. L. CATLING, Proprietor.

Good Open and

Close Carriages

to Let on

Hire.

Furnished

Apartments

for

Coachman.

SUSSEX & HARDWICK MEWS

(Near St. Saviour's and Presbyterian Churches),

WISH ROAD, EASTBOURNE.

W. H. WOOD,

Job-master and Livery Stable Keeper,

HORSES TAKEN at LIVERY. GOOD LOOSE BOXES for HUNTERS

Saddle Horses and Quiet Ponies for Children. . .

. Riding and Driving Lessons given by Proprietor.

1. **Before the advent of the horse drawn omnibus public transport was limited to hire carriages affordable only to the most wealthy inhabitants of Eastbourne.**

Uckfield and East Grinstead. At the same time the "Hero" provided the Brighton to Hastings service. It left The Anchor, Seahouses just after midday also calling at the New Inn and The Lamb at Old Town then proceeding to Brighton via Seaford and Newhaven on Tuesdays, Thursdays and Saturdays. On its return on Monday, Wednesday and Friday it went through Pevensey and Bexhill back to Hastings.

As most transport in the early 1800's relied upon horse power, equine related trades numbered large amongst Eastbourne artisans. The farrier, Thomas Baker, was based at Sea Houses whilst saddlers and wheelwrights were concentrated around South Street. However some traditional industry survived in the town, for instance in Meads lived Thomas Luck a lime burner. It was perhaps his son who ran the Mead's omnibus service at the end of the century. Meanwhile those visiting the town for its seaside restorative powers could attend Sarah Webb's "warm and shower baths".

2. One of Bradfords Omnibuses at the Leaf Hall in Seaside. Circa 1870s.

As the development of Eastbourne as a resort progressed, roads were built to replace the muddy paths, by 1866 the original station (near the Post Office) was

Established 1858.

Telephone No. 84.   Telegrams—"Tamden, Eastbourne."

CHAPMAN & SONS,

Jobmasters,

Proprietors of the Vigilant Coach, Brighton and Eastbourne.

Stage Coaches Horsed by Contract.

RIDING AND DRIVING ESTABLISHMENT.

Queen's Mews, Cavendish Place,

. . AND . .

Victoria Mews, Susans Road.

Largest Livery Stables on the South Coast.

LIVERY AND HUNTING STABLES.

Every attention given to Hunters at Livery.

CARRIAGES OF EVERY DESCRIPTION ON HIRE.

COACHES, DRAGS, Etc.

Lessons in Four-in-Hand and Tamden Driving by the Proprietors.

Horses of Good Quality for Saddle or Harness.

Single Brougham and Victoria Horses.

Well-Matched Pairs, with or without Carriages.

GOOD SADDLE HORSES FOR LADIES OR GENTLEMEN.

Well Conditioned Hunters up to Weight.

LEAPING LESSONS AT LANGNEY FARM.

Ten Minutes from Eastbourne.

Special Terms to Schools.   *Children Carefully Taught.*

HORSES TRIED OVER FENCES. 10/6.

CHAPMAN & SONS, Cavendish Place.

3. In addition to stage carriage work Chapman provided many other equestrian services. The extent of these is evident from contemporary advertisements.

replaced by another wooden structure to the east, on the site of the present station. This enabled Upperton Road to connect with Grove Road and Terminus Road, which had been laid in 1850. Around the middle of the century F. Bradford established himself as a fly proprietor with premises in Susans Road and Victoria Place. In addition to his activities providing carriages for hire, it appears that he also ran one of the first regular horse omnibuses, one of which is seen here in the 1870s at the Leaf Hall, Seaside.

About eight years after the railway came to Eastbourne, William Chapman and his family arrived in the town occupying a succession of premises starting in Old Town. Chapman created what was to become not only the largest carriage operation in Eastbourne but, by the turn of the century, was the largest ratepayer.

Chapman and his sons soon established extensive interests in the development of the town and frequently came up against the Council particularly when it proposed restrictions on hackney carriage operations. Regulations for the hackney trade applied to horse omnibuses and were governed by rules drawn up by the local watch committee.

A typical confrontation occured one night in 1880 at the Carpenters Arms in Terminus Road when Chapman and fellow operators met in opposition to new regulations which would require each driver to display a badge some 3"x2". Despite lengthy speeches, threats and a good moan washed down no doubt by several pints, their voice was ignored and each driver thereafter wore his badge. This practice (which continued until 1989) was extended to conductors as we shall see later. In 1882 the population had reached 22000, the town achieved borough status and growing popularity required another rebuild of the railway station (and extension

4. By the turn of the century, outings on Chapmans Stage Coaches were exercises in nostalgia as this mode of transport was rendered obsolete with the spread of the railways.

in 1886 to its present shape). The station was the focus for bus services which stopped outside the Gildridge Hotel. It was also around this time that suggestions of a narrow gauge tram to Pevensey were muted.

By 1882 William Chapman's enterprises had expanded again, he was running the "Vigilant" coach between Eastbourne and Brighton as well as offering riding lessons, horse livery and carriage hire. In about 1882 be commenced his omnibus service, or "bus" as the term became abbreviated. These services encompassed the main areas of population such as The Archery (for the East End and Norway), Old Town, Ocklynge and Meads. Chapmans fleet of seven buses would have been drawn by two horses, the type in this view has knifeboard seating running the length of the upper deck.

5. **This single deck omnibus standing outside the Gildredge Hotel is of the type known as the "knifeboard" due to its seating arrangement with one seat running the length of the upper deck. On these early double deck buses the spiral staircase had yet to appear.**

There was apparently sufficient traffic to attract other operators such as G. Luck from 1887, based at the Ship Hotel stables Meads, and G.S.Prismall, details of whom are scarce but he was still trying to obtain licences as late as 1902. Bradford had taken up other trade but had some interest in bus operation until late in the century. In addition to omnibus services, fly or cab operators also ran several excursions from the seafront, these centered upon the pier which was completed in 1872. Chapman established a ticket office at the pier entrance just down the road from his headquarters in Victoria Place (now part of Terminus Road). The most popular vehicles were wagonettes which had stepped seating and were either open or had a canopy. This was the type of body used on the early motor char-a-bancs.

Over 100 hackney carriages were licensed in the borough in 1893 but few were buses unlike big neighbour Brighton where buses were already causing traffic chaos by the 1880s. Cab operators in Eastbourne were well provided for, a splendid canopy being constructed at the station and shelters were located around the town. The cost of hiring hackney carriages was very high and the bus was frequently used by skilled artisans and the middle-classes but was still relatively expensive - the poor just walked!

6. **Wagonettes still found plenty of work in Eastbourne during the Edwardian era, in this case providing excursions for day trippers who would have arrived by train.**

Carriages, bath chair attendants, porters etc all fell within the system of licensing. Special stands were allocated to each from where they could ply for trade, these pitches were marked by cast metal plates mounted near the pavement. The last type of plate introduced was for the motor charabanc. Examples of these were found around the grounds of the Grand Hotel and on the walls surrounding the Wish Tower. Replicas of the plates can be found in the town's local history museum.

Failure to comply with the licensing laws was dealt with by the magistrates. In 1902 a Chapman conductor, Edward Steadman of Seaside was summoned for acting as an unlicensed driver. His defence that he was actually conducting was dismissed, as a conductor was considered a driver in law and the Bench imposed a fine of 2s 6d.

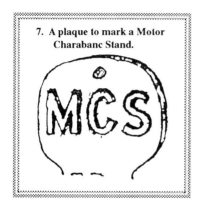

7. **A plaque to mark a Motor Charabanc Stand.**

We have few accounts of the life of the ordinary bus crew although it seems that many of Chapmans employees had long careers with the company. For Chapman, business was also a pastime and though his stagecoach had suffered competition from the railway it continued to run allbeit less frequently. Towards the end of the century he organised special journeys aboard his coach, which were widely reported in the press. Early photographs recorded these events and Chapman drove his teams to Brighton and

London for what must by then have been the nostalgic appeal of older inhabitants.

Many of the conductors were young men taken on for the seasonal work on the wagonette excursions. If they did well, they were retained for winter duties on the buses. Unemployment was quite high as many men were being discharged from service in the army following the conclusion of the war in South Africa. It was one such man, George Button of Roselands Cottages, a private in the 3rd (Militia) Battalion of the Royal Sussex Regiment who in September 1902 appeared before the magistrates. Presiding was the mayor, Alderman Neville Strange. Button was charged with assault on John Reed, conductor on Chapmans buses. Reed's bus was about to leave the Archery terminus for the station, Reed popped into the Hotel to relieve himself when he was accosted by Button who pestered him for the price of a pint. Reed told him where to go and received a punch in the face, as he staggered out of the hotel his driver William Winchester witnessed the injury and heard what had happened. With this testimony the case was found proved and Button fined 4s 6d which seems quite a light sentence considering the standard fine for not having a light on a bicycle was 2s 6d. Despite Eastbourne's reputation as an affluent resort, violence was common place, not only amongst the working people but by wealthy youths. The lager louts of yesteryear hung around the promenades and hurled insults and abuse at visitors. Special patrols had to be organised by the watch committee to combat this menace.

The religious lobby anxious to protect the moral welfare of the fly drivers campaigned for many years against the need for them to work on Sundays. However everyone involved in the seasonal holiday trade worked a seven day week but by the end of the century late Victorian morals and the dislike of noisy motor buses found a ban in place on buses along with bands and bathing on Sundays.

In 1899 Messers Jury and Son started to operate motor taxis which no doubt attracted the attentions of curious onlookers and the approbation of the genteel folk who had sought retirement in tranquility. These new vehicles were probably bodied locally and finished to a standard which matched any horse conveyance, but they did cause clouds of dust and frightened the horses. It seems that a premium over usual fares was charged for a ride in such a novel style.

The subject of charges seems to have been the source of continued grievance amongst travellers in the town, despite supposedly fixed prices for distance, the coachmen were apt to charge according to demand. Thus fares to lodging houses in the more distant east end of town were highest when a train arrived from the metropolis in midsummer. If by good fortune (for the coachman) it happened to rain the price would rise again. Chapman had made an unusual decision regarding fares on his buses, they were fixed according to the route and not to the distance travelled, thus journeys within hilly Old Town were 3d but if you wanted to go down as far as the Leaf Hall the fare remained the same. Moreover, the fare on the short but affluent Meads route was set at 2d. Passengers were well aware of the system used elsewhere but Chapman claimed that this enabled him to make sufficient profit to maintain his network throughout the year, although later when faced with

Corporation motor buses, he claimed that he had run much of the service for the public convenience at a loss to himself.

The die seemed cast, frequent letters were appearing in the local papers complaining of Chapmans antiquated buses, their unpunctuality, high fares and overcrowding. Chapmans buses were indeed old, his coach building activities perhaps employed more profitably elsewhere. The fifteen minute service on the main cross town route may have coped off season but was hopelessly stretched in the summer. Another situation which was blamed upon the operation but wasn't of his choosing was the council's decision to allocate specific points where buses could pick up and put down passengers, these being marked by enamelled signs affixed to lamps, trees or walls. This alleviated the suffering of the horses whose lives were shortened by the constant strain of pulling away. The fixing of the signs caused ruffled feathers amongst the gentry in Meads and Upperton, each wanted the stops placed somewhere other than outside their house.

If the new regulations were enforced by the constables with their usual enthusiam, it was not suprising that Chapmans conductors shook their heads as they rumbled past prospective passengers. This seemed like the final insult and a long suffering public agitated for something more modern and reliable. The life of Chapmans crews must have been arduous, long hours in all weathers continually exposed to the elements aboard unheated, rattling vehicles all for less than £1 a week, which must have made crime a constant temptation.

A luckless duo of Chapmans employees were Frank Bourne, conductor, and driver George Winchester. Bourne was a young man employed in the spring and retained whilst Winchester had been in the company for nine years. One afternoon Nora Kirk, a school teacher, boarded their bus at the recreation ground, Seaside, heading for the station. Later she realised she had lost her purse. Returning home she boarded the same bus and asked the conductor if a purse had been found - indeed it had, Isabel Boys a domestic servant of Seaside Road had found it on the return journey and handed it to conductor Bourne. Instead of passing it over to Chapmans office or the police, he sold the purse to Winchester the driver for 12s, it contained a gold guinea, some change and a postal order. Winchester kept the change and burnt the remainder. When police apprehended him at Chapmans stables later in the day, a hapless crew confessed and received a sentence of one months hard labour. Occurrences such as this did little to enhance the already tarnished reputation of the bus service. Chapman himself was no stranger to court whether as witness or complainant. The local legal profession must have done well from the constant stream of litigation which arose from his business and seemed common amongst all trades.

A popular excursion by wagonette was through the fields to Hampden Park which had been purchased for the town in 1902 at a cost of £3000. That year was one of celebration with a new monarch and Boer War ended. A contingent of Indian troops visited Eastbourne, crowds gathered along Grove Road to meet them off the train. The Viceroy's Bodyguard, Lancers and Sikhs were later treated to a drive around the town in a fleet of Chapman's horse charabancs.

In response to complaints about transport in the town the Corporation gained powers to run its own bus service. The search for suitable vehicles for the Council's proposed motor bus service was not without controversy. Advertisements were duly placed in the trade press inviting tenders for vehicles seating at least 16. In considering the response the sub-committee deemed it nescessary to undertake a number of visits over the length and breadth of the country. They considered the proposals on Milnes Daimler, Thorneycroft, City and Suburban and Stirling. Products could be tested at the Auto-Car exhibition at Crystal Palace and at a similar show in Edinburgh, vehicles in service were also to be inspected in London and Kent. These perambulations raised eyebrows amongst other councillors who suggested that manufactures could simply send samples to be tried within the borough.

The wandering sub-committee seem to have been kept in check and they finally examined vehicles. First was a Stirling 12 seater, 12 h.p. which was seen running from Oxford Circus to Cricklewood, carrying about 400 passengers a day. It was reported to produce considerable vibration and engine noise. Secondly was a Milnes Daimler 32 seater, 16 h.p. double decker which was inspected in service with Skinners at Hastings, it having also been seen at the Crystal Palace exhibition. Finally the City and Suburban Electric Carriage Co offered a petrol/electric vechicle but had none available for demonstration. Anxious to explore all avenues the sub-committee took a ride in a petrol electric motor car and were impressed with its smooth running and freedom from vibration, however lacking any prototype or firm plans for construction, this type was excluded from the short list.

The final choice lay between a 14 seater Stirling at £683 or the Milnes Daimler at £750 also seating 14, the Daimler having the advantage of 4 extra h.p. and better tyres. What probably clinched it forMilnes Daimler was the widespread reports of the success of the Hasting vehicle (which was a double deck open top bus). The arrival of such a vehicle was awaited with anticipation in Eastbourne. Unknown to most people was that Milnes Daimler couldn't supply double deckers until the winter thus a 14 seater, single decker was hired. The initial disappointment was soon overcome. On Thursday 10th April 1903 various council officials and their families went for an excursion aboard the new bus to Hampden Park. For the rest of the day and on Friday people enjoyed rides aboard the new bus, finally at 10.20am on the Saturday it left the railway station and commenced its first fare paying service with a route which led down Terminus Road to the seafront, then up to the Pilot and back again to the station via Meads, the outward journey taking 15 minutes, the return 8.

The prospect of a tramway system appearing in Eastbourne conflicted with the planned opulence of the town, although the working people at least fully expected that they would benefit from the latest forms of transport. In an effort to forstall tramways and in face of what was patently an inadequate horse bus operation the

Corporation had included powers to operate its own services in the Eastbourne Bill which had obtained parliamentary consent in 1902. The excitement of the debate which carried on even after the first Corporation motor buses started running is difficult to measure from the pages of the old newspaper print, the headlines of the age having nothing of the drama seen today. What is apparent is that there were two very different perspectives over the need for trams. One was that of the wealthy classes living in Upperton and Meads who wanted nothing of tracks, overhead wires and the like, the other, wholeheartely in support of trams was the working class view of the East End. Artisans and labourers, tradesmen and domestics travelled from as far as Fort Road with only spasmodic motor buses to be caught at the Archery.

8. The first Milnes Daimler motor buses proved a disappointment to the public who had been waiting for a double deck bus similar to that running in Hastings.

Whatever the debate over motor buses, the general effect of motorised transport was just too much for some of the towns elderly residents. Mrs Philson, a lady of advanced years, tripped over her long skirts after being frightened by the approach of a motor, a conveyance of which she had a dread. She did, we are told, survive her ordeal, but the roads around town certainly were not adequate. Mrs Philson's experience outside the Gildredge Hotel was on an unmade road, only pathed crossings protected the pedestrian from mud and horse droppings. The crossings themselves made for spectacular displays as the buses lurched over them sending passengers sprawling.

It was a good thing that the Corporation had started with a light single deck bus as no serious consideration had been given to the type of tyre (solid) which sould be used. The unexpected cost of constant renewal detracted from profits. After one week, a generally good impression had been gained by the smooth running although some people maintained they would walk rather than travel inside the stuffy saloon. Other reservations arose with the speeds obtained, the driver was obviously getting the hang of things when exceeding 20 mph down Meads Hill, dodging horse carts on the way.

It was agreed with Milnes Daimler that the vehicle on hire be purchased along with a second to be supplied. The next bus arrived on May 30th and was at first placed on service to Hampden Park, a pleasant excursion across open fields, this didn't last long and it was soon placed on the Upperton - Archery route in competition with Chapmans horse buses. A shortage of fuel curtailed its activities until arrangements could be made for additional supplies. Garaging was at first in the open air adjacent to the Susans Road premises which housed the dust carts. Temporary "stabling" was arranged under cover whilst a permanent building was put up at Roselands.

Just who was to blame for the fiascos experienced with the first motor buses? Recriminations flowed freely in the press and at council meetings. Motions were passed, investigations made and inspectors appointed, the great calamity was nothing less than the collapse of the town's transport system, a situation which improved little throughout the coming winter. What had gone wrong? For a start Chapman obviously saw the end in sight, his buses made up only a small portion of his business, his vehicles were worn out and investment in motors against Corporation services would have been unwise. The Council had already snubbed him when planning their service despite all his years of experience. The horse buses may have been slow and the windows rattled but at least they tended to turn up when expected. The Corporation's bus service was an enterprise outside the experience of any council official, the vehicles themselves were in their infancy, details such as shelter, maintenance, tyres and fuel had been given little regard. When the railway reached Eastbourne the LBSCR had already gained experience in such matters as timetabling. The mechanics of the steam engine were well understood, its fuel readily available unlike petroleum.

No sooner had the first hired Milnes Daimler taken to the road than Chapman retaliated by cutting back services, for instance the Archery route was severed at the Leaf Hall leaving hundreds of passengers with a long walk. Chapmans justified these moves by the need to cut costs and maintain profits in the face of competition. Revenge was a more likely motive, he just couldn't get out of the business quick enough from then on. Although the initial reaction of the East Enders was to petition in favour of the old horse buses, public opinion soon clamoured for trams. By the time the last Chapmans horse bus ran on 29th August 1903 they had become irrelevent. The ancient horse bus bodies along with the horses were auctioned off on September 1st at the Victoria Mews, the bodies going for less than £10 each, many destined for bungalow town, Shoreham.

One wry letter in the paper asked whether the British Museum had been given the opportunity to purchase them!

Thus after just five months running, the motor bus almost had the road to itself. Luck's Meads service apparently ran at least until summer 1904 and many photos attributed to Chapmans probably relate to Luck's Buses. Chapman had lowered fares in face of those charges on the motors, but the Corporation faced with unforseen running costs soon raised theirs later in the year. Our narrative has run a little ahead though, before the end of horse buses a great public meeting took place at the recreation ground, Seaside. A notable abscence was that of Chapman. The debate was over the future travel arrangements for the East End of the town. Reporters from the local press were hemmed in by the crowds which may have numbered a thousand, although many were children watching the spectacle. Various speakers, including councillors, discussed the chronic condition of the motor buses and the question of trams. The only operator present was Luck of the Meads route, although he heckled well he was less eloquent when given the floor. The meeting drew up proposals to be put before the Council and subsequently routes for a tramway were drawn up, discussed, costed etc. Arguments raged over which roads would be covered, but all the time the tramway question was very gently being eased aside. It is futile to list all the schemes which were put forward, conduits, overhead, stud contact, the routes, the fares, all became one great might have been.

Corporation motor bus journeys were often lost due to mechanical failures, with the Archery bus often being withdrawn in favour of the Meads route, if either vehicle was off the road. This was happening against the continued agitation for trams on the East End. Meads residents apparently had less use for their bus in the evenings when it was sent to supplement the Upperton route. Much to the disgust of the residents the next motor bus deliveries were yet another pair of 14 seater single deck Milnes Daimlers, but already thoughts had turned to steam traction. In Torquay, Clarkson steam buses were receiving favourable reports whilst in Eastbourne, Milnes Daimler had to send down their own mechanics to sort out the ailing fleet.

By August 1903 the arrival of additional vehicles and the demise of horse buses made another route possible, this time running from the Lamb Hotel to the Archery. With the fleet housed at Roselands, fuel storage was increased to 1000 gallons, additional clerical staff were engaged and conductors wages increased from 18s to £1 a week. Sidney Walters, a driver, was cautioned for furious driving and the staff warned that if anyone was found guilty of traffic offences they would be dismissed.

One of the Clarkson steam buses of the type running in Torquay was demonstrated in Eastbourne. It was a 10-seat tourer but other types were quoted for. There was general consternation when the council and public found that the much praised steam bus was to be yet another single decker. A feature of the steam bus was the reduced maintenance required. Water was heated by a paraffin burner, and stored in tanks beneath the seats. Its initial sucess saw a second Clarkson on order due early in 1904.

The winter months finally saw the arrival of the first double decker which relieved the strain upon resources, in fact a popular winter pastime had been watching the broken down buses in the streets.

9. One of the first double deckers, a 20 hp Milnes Daimler makes progress along the centre of the road amidst horse droppings.

One of the first double deck Milnes Daimlers, the 20hp model which had a Daimler chassis and Milnes body which was marketed as a complete unit. The bus is making progress along the crest of the road, a practice made common by the steep camber required to provide adequate drainage. The buildings along the promenade are basically the same as in modern times although the addition of sun lounges and lobbies to hotels has destroyed the unity of style. The popular ride from the Reboubt to the foot of Beachy Head had originally been served by horse buses, nearly a century later the route has lost none of its appeal.

When the requirement for vehicles to be registered was enacted at the end of 1903, the Milnes Daimlers received the numbers AP289, 291/3/5. The use of odd numbers was to become a feature of the fleet. Early vehicles were finished in red/cream with brown trim. Their interiors were like Victorian funeral parlours with coffin like bodies with velvet curtains and were very unpopular. By 1907 all had received new charabanc or "observation" bodies intended for use on the seafront services, these being built locally by W. Gibbons. The old bodies minus glass and fittings were sold to W. Eridge for use as bathing huts. Three of the original Daimlers were eventually used for spares after withdrawal in 1908 but No 2 (AP 293) lasted until 1913 in service as a sanitary department lorry.

As originally delivered the Milnes Daimlers had seating for two passengers beside the driver and another on the rear platform, use of these seats was however prohibited by the Chief Constable.

On the Milnes Damiler double deckers, upper deck passengers were not permitted along Church Street and to enforce this rule No.6 had its stairs removed in 1906! Shortly before withdrawal in 1908 it received experimental petrol electric controls. The second double deck Daimler arrived at the end of 1904. It later received a replacement body from Gibbons and was in turn converted to a lorry. The lorry body itself was placed on No 30 acquired in 1910 and served in this form from 1911 until 1924.

10. Members of the Motor Omnibus department pose in front of AP2009, a 25 hp Milnes Daimler of 1905.

One of the 1905 Milnes Daimlers, possibly No 10 (AP 2009), was the first of the 24hp versions and it had a conventional radiator design as opposed to the coal scuttle type on previous deliveries. The large fleet name against a cream background relieves the sombre brown paintwork. The bus had a relatively short life of five years. The sideboard for Hampden Park indicates the summer season when there were 12 journeys a day to this popular destination.

Coporation bus timetables were published from the outset and have continued to be updated throughout the 90 year history of the undertaking, although the sense of permanency which permitted enamelled timetables has not endured. A variety of local printers produced the timetables which up to 1906 were issued monthly before settling down to a seasonal format. Early issues included a small map of places served, together with fares. Tickets could be pre-purchased at a discount, reduced rates being in operation on certain routes between 8 and 9am. The first bus left the Archery for the station at 7.45am, last buses ran around 11pm. Passengers on the 1d trip from the station to Old Town were still forbidden to ride on upper decks after the Lamb Inn.

There were six basic services with the Old Town/Ocklynge route already interworked. Frequencies were reflected by the small size of the fleet, but with the arrival of De Dion Boutons, services on the main routes increased to every 10 minutes. Certain journeys to Hampden Park and the Foot of Beachy Head were liable to cancellation in poor weather. Passengers were not allowed to smoke in the saloon and dogs were not carried. Advertising helped defray printing costs.

Anyone unfortunate enough to leave luggage on a bus was charged 2d for its recovery.

Steam buses, like other contemporary innovations such as petrol electrics, were generally short lived, in Eastbourne the hard chalky water soon rendering the Clarkson steam buses inoperable. Numbered 4 and 5 they entered the fleet in 1903/04 respectively. Seating 17 they were finished in polished wood and had celestory roofs. They required frequent top ups of water, drivers often making illegal use of the many horse troughs. Hydrants were situated around the town where bowsers filled up and then sprinkled surfaces in an attempt to lay the dust.

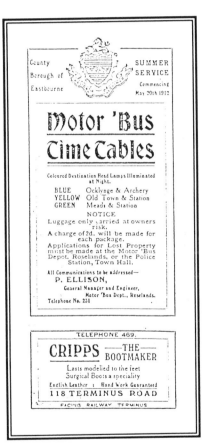

11. A summer service timetable for 1912; earlier timetables had been issued monthly such had been the rate of changes as services developed.

Further Milnes Daimlers were received in 1905/06 giving another 6 double deckers, one of which, No 14, is seen at Hampden Park gates and again in Terminus Road. No 9 was subject to an interesting experiment in 1905 when it received a cover on the top deck. This was soon removed on safety grounds. The last Milnes survived until 1917.

The cream upper panels on the double deckers for a time bore the legend "Eastbourne Corporation" but were soon replaced by revenue earning enamelled advertisements. Slip boards along the sides of the lower saloon were eventually replaced by short lived destination boards above the drivers canopy. These in turn were replaced by the destination box, this being the forerunner of modern electronic systems.

The steam buses were withdrawn in 1906 and in June of that year passed to the Torquay Road Car Co Ltd whose vehicles had originally so impressed the

21

Eastbourne officials. When Percy Ellison arrived from Leeds in 1906 to manage the fleet, he set about smartening up what was a floundering organisation. Crews were provided with proper uniforms and soon the undertaking was able to produce its own football team and social club.

Purchases of new vehicles were often restricted by the limited output of factories. During the period 1907-10 the corporation purchased 17 secondhand French De Dions. The second batch of three which arrived from Associated Omnibus Co Ltd of London in December 1908 were probably already painted in the new livery of Navy blue and Yellow. The Dions seated 32 and had 24 h.p. engines which must have been quite reliable as most lasted until the end of the WWI.

→
12. Milnes Daimler No 14 is seen on a seasonal working to Hampden Park.

↓ **13. The same bus is seen in a rear view in Terminus Road.**

Until the purchase of the ex Demonstrator Leyland Cub in 1968 only seven buses had run in the fleet with non-local registrations. Four were Leylands from Wellingborough and the others amongst a batch of ten purchased secondhand from the Associated Omnibus Co Ltd in 1910 (the rest were re-registered). No 30 (LC 29 57) was by far the shortest lived of these, new in 1905 it had just over a years service.

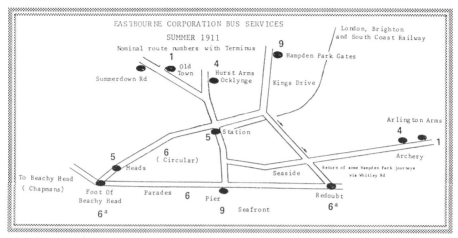

EASTBOURNE CORPORATION BUS SERVICES

SUMMER 1911

Nominal route numbers with Terminus

London, Brighton and South Coast Railway

Hampden Park Gates

Old Town — Summerdown Rd

Hurst Arms — Ocklynge

Kings Drive

Arlington Arms

Station

Meads — (Circular)

Archery

Seaside

Return of some Hampden Park journeys via Whitley Rd

To Beachy Head (Chapmans)

Foot Of Beachy Head

Parades

Pier

Redoubt

Seafront

1911 there are still only three all year round services supplemented in the summer season by the promenade, circular and Hampden Park journeys. The route numbers shown were not carried but can be related to the service numbers first allocated in the 1940s.

No 30 is heading past the railway station bound for Ocklynge There was a frequent headway with up to 11 buses an hour although the route network still only boasted three year round services. The system comprised Archery / Ocklynge / Old Town and Station-Meads but one trip an hour on the Ocklynge working was extended to the Arlington Arms beyond the Archery terminus.

14. Shortlived bus No 30 is heading past the railway station bound for Ocklynge.

The last of the Milnes Daimlers to be received was No 14 (AP 2019) which was new in 1906. In picture 15 it has just stopped after turning into Seaside Road by what is now the Army & Navy store but for many years was Barkers. By 1917 the body had been removed from No 14 and was placed on one of the Leyland S types purchased from the Wellingborough Motor Omnibus Co Ltd. The outbreak of war curtailed the Anglo German partnership but by this time Leyland was expanding its production. Note the drive mechanism and the radiator which was of normal pattern rather than the coal scuttle type of the original Daimlers.

No 14 is heading either for the Archery or the Arlington Arms, the last marking the eastern limit of operations at the time. Note how destinations revolved around public house names!

15. No 14 (AP2019) heading into Seaside on its way to the Archery.

One of the ex Associated Omnibus Co Ltd De Dions is seen heading along Seaside Road on the 10 minute service to Old Town. No 25 (AP 2033) was reregistered on acquisition, originally new 1905/06 it was purchased by Eastbourne in 1910. It is the summer of 1914 and the vehicle has gained several enamelled advertisements in its four years service. Although the driver still has no protection against the elements developments do include a destination box. This particular bus lasted until 1918, after which it served as a lorry with the Borough surveyors department until 1924. Just like the practice on tram cars the lower saloon quarter lights carry adverts, in an age without television or radio any opportunity for advertising display was taken.

16. Purchased secondhand in 1910 this De Dion No 25 (AP2033) received its local registration after acquisition.

2. EARLY ROUTES

Although there were no numbers or letters to distinguish routes, the earliest vehicles were easily identified by the large boards with route details along their sides, vehicles generally stayed on the same route. At night, lamps were carried with coloured glass which indicated the main routes as below

Blue - Ocklynge

Yellow - Old Town

Green - Meads

Just how reliable this was or how long it lasted is not recorded. This basic route pattern formed the backbone of services until WWI, the only real development was the introduction of seasonal services to Hampden Park and along the parades together with some circular tours taking in the seafront. In the winter the Carew Road area was served from the station although these were incorporated in the Hampden Park schedule when the service became year round. Frequencies on the main routes from the station were about 8 to 15 minutes, but Meads was 30. Some of the Archery services were extended hourly to the Arlington Arms, then the Lodge and eventually to Langney.

The war years brought many problems, the consequences for services being overall reduction in all but the main routes and less journeys on these. The routes which operated throughout WWI were the Archery to Ocklynge and Old Town services together with the Meads bus, only occasional Lodge to Carew Road buses supplemented this very basic provision which barely matched the horse routes surrendered by Chapman and Luck eleven years previously.

The wartime fleet consisted mainly of De Dion-Bouton 24hp 32 seaters which had been purchased second hand in 1910, plus a quartet of rather dated Milnes Daimlers of 1906 vintage. Only two Leyland B Types of 1912 represented current designs.

The carefree passengers seemed oblivious to the war raging across the Channel although posters in the windows extol the requirements of home defence. Rules regarding the seating of passengers by the driver had been abandoned and the crew sported uniforms which include a white great coat for the driver. The lack of adverts betrays the recent arrival of No 33 (HC 589) but the B type chassis was much in demand for war use and the batch which had arrived in the spring spent just a few summer months in service before requisition by the war department in August 1914. The 38 seater bodies were set aside and when the conditions allowed the release of the Leyland S3 war subsidy chassis the Corporation purchased three, one of which received the body from No 33 in 1916. Future rebodying to single deck by the Corporation prolonged the life of the "new" No 33 until the mid thirties. Seen here about to leave the Pier for the foot of Beachy Head, such routes would soon be abandoned with the loss of vehicles. Note the speed restriction on the lower panel which remained at 12 mph!

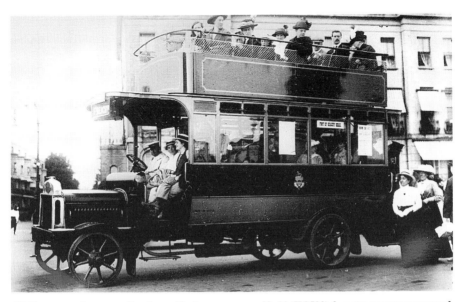

17. War was raging across the channel but passengers on No 33 (HC589) do not seem very concerned.

A small number of war subsidy buses became available during the course of the conflict. Eastbourne managed to obtain three in 1916, numbered 33-5 (HC 1153/55/57) they received bodies from the 1914 "B" types.

The only vehicles purchased during the war were four second hand Leylands acquired from Wellingborough Motor Omnibus Co Ltd, these dating from 1912. Although they were probably delivered with their original bodies these had not been requested and were replaced with bodies off Milnes Daimlers or De Dions. Substantial rebodying to single deck configuration in 1922 also coincided with their re-registration.

After the war a long period of Leyland domination commenced which would last until the 1930s, the fleet having survived its difficult start and the trials of war under the steady hand of Percy Ellison, now restructuring and expansion of routes were priorities.

Although the horse bus soon succumbed to motor buses for stage carriage work within the town, lines of wagonettes or brakes still formed outside the pier as they collected passengers on excursions or outings. Perhaps some of Chapmans wagonettes are heading for the Downs on a Sunday School treat. Corporation buses operating along the seafront bore the destination of Beachy Head, a claim hotly contested by Chapmans in July 1907 when they pointed out to the Council that Corporation buses merely ran to the Foot of Beachy Head. Hires and excursions would be the mainstay of all small operators in the town until modern times

18. The First World War was to see the end of horse drawn passenger traffic. Fuel and vehicle shortages kept up the demand during the hostilities but in rural Sussex, where horse omnibuses still served several stations, the end was close.

Chapmans was a family business founded upon entrepreneurial ideas in the best spirit of the age. During WWI a number of vehicles were converted to run on gas overcoming fuel rationing, as not only the Chapman family depended upon the business but his drivers and mechanics were loyal long service employees. William Chapman would stand by the pier handing out leaflets promoting his excursions and his pale primrose vehicles formed lines down Victoria Place (now the bottom of Terminus Road). An efficient system of ticketing was developed enabling rapid loading at a location like the pier where police enforced strict time limits on waiting.

19. Always at the forefront of passenger transport developments, Chapman was quick to augment rationed fuel by the use of gas carried in huge bags above the coaches.

20. A complicated system of ticketing was used by Chapman. Accurate identification of vehicles and passengers booked on trips was essential, as the police were quick to move on any coach overstaying its allotted standing time.

21. By 1911 Chapmans tours had reached Scotland and Cornwall. International agreements saw his operations spread to the continent in the 1920s.

3. THE INTER-WAR YEARS

The story of Chapmans coaches provides a link in the first thirty years of bus operations in the town. Forced to withdraw from stage carriage work Wm Chapman purchased his first motor charabanc in 1909 and by 1921 had built up a fleet of 36 vehicles consisting of 24 Dennis, 4 AEC, 6 Tilling Stevens and 2 Belsize. These operated long distance tours as well as local excursions, the first tours in 1911 reaching Lands End and Scotland. Roads were still narrow and traffic light. A novel device was fitted to Chapmans coaches to warn the driver of traffic wishing to overtake. A bell was operated by passengers seated at the rear alerting the driver or attracting the attention of the gentlemen guide who accompanied each tour. Such was the esteem in which the business was held that several hoteliers used by the company took out shares in the coach business when it became a limited company in 1920.

Chapman regularly travelled on his own tours ensuring standards were maintained. In 1922 agreement between European countries made overseas coach tours possible. Chapmans then ranged from the West of Ireland to Italy. By 1927 his fleet had grown to 37, all Dennis vehicles. His head office was on the corner of Terminus Road/Seaside Road, facing what is now the co-op store where boards similar to those used at rail stations advertised the days excursions to places such as Pevensey, Rye, Seaford or Alfriston. There were competitors such as Bassett & Co but Chapman seemed to go from strength to strength.

22. Gretna Green, a regular stop on Chapmans tours to Scotland. By 1927 the fleet was entirely of Dennis manufacture. With a fleet of 37, standardisation reduced running costs.

23. The prices may have changed but the destinations remain popular with visitors over sixty years later. Chapman had regained stage carriage status in conjunction with Pickfords on the London motor coach service.

Regular rail services to the capital were provided by the LBSCR, 14s/3d (71p) buying a third class return which took just under 1½ hours from Eastbourne to London. During the summer months Chapman in conjunction with Pickfords established a motor coach service via East Grinstead. The London terminus was the Grosvenor Hotel, Victoria and passengers were allowed 14lb of luggage.

Although some horse brake trips survived into the twenties, journeys to the delights of Wannock tea gardens etc would soon be the preserve of the motor coach. The firm experimented with chassis makes such as Maudsley and Lancias the fleet reaching a peak of 50 vehicles. The 160 shareholders received reasonable dividends on their investments and the company was a source of pride to the town.

24. Chapmans fleet reached a peak of fifty vehicles, the demand for his excursions and tours seemed endless. The Chapman family were justifiably proud of their success but the heady summers of the interwar years would end quite soon.

No 4 of the second series (HC 1447) was from a batch of six Leyland 32 seat single deckers delivered in 1919 with bodies completed by Vickers to a Leyland design. Less substantial than their successors, the PLSC Lions had their lives extended by rebuilding within the Corporation workshops, work which apparently left them unaltered, other than a change to pneumatic tyres by the mid 20s. No. 4 survived until 1936 by which time exposed cab sides were outmoded as was the practice of passengers sitting alongside the driver. Even on a bright day both driver and conductor benefited from their uniforms, buses remaining unheated and draughty. No 40 (HC 1451) was also withdrawn in 1936 surviving with the Corporation as a lorry until 1940.

Recovery from WWI saw the gradual expansion of services which included the introduction of a Devonshire Park to Ocklynge route running every half hour, No 4 waits at its terminus but by the end of the decade Devonshire Park services were diverted to Old Town. Other services to Ocklynge included journeys via Carew Road to the Hurst Arms and the Archery service, with a five minute frequency increased to meet demand as required. Trips from the East End were later divided leaving Whitley Road or the Archery every ten minutes.

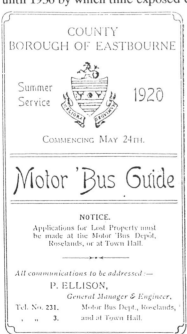

COUNTY
BOROUGH OF EASTBOURNE

Summer
Service　　　　　　1920

COMMENCING MAY 24TH.

Motor Bus Guide

NOTICE.

Applications for Lost Property must be made at the Motor 'Bus Depôt, Roselands, or at Town Hall.

All communications to be addressed :—

P. ELLISON,

General Manager & Engineer,

Tel. No. 231.　　Motor Bus Dept., Roselands,
　　,, 3.　　and at Town Hall.

Gowland Bros., Printers, Eastbourne.

25. The 1920s were a period for rebuilding the Corporation bus fleet, services in the 1920s barely matched pre World War I levels until new vehicles were available.

26. No 40 (HC1451) was not withdrawn until 1936 and even then it survived a further four years with the Corporation as a lorry.

From a fading sepia photograph this view was taken while on layover at the Redoubt with the driver posed against the bulk of No 33 (HC 1153). The bus is a Leyland War Subsidy S3 with a body which had been transfered from one of the 1914 B types requisitioned by the War Department. The wheel discs and high radiator identify this product of WWI, which along with two others survived to receive a rebuild in the Coporations workshops in the late 20s which saw them emerge as single deckers.

Summer seafront services in the early twenties saw a basic 10 minute Parade service, with extras as required. The Hampden Park run still started from the pier and circular tours which took in the seafront, ran about six times a day.

It wasn't until the late 1920s that any innovation in bus design was evident in new deliveries to the fleet but the Corporations own workshops continued to experiment and produced a bus fitted with Upper deck windscreen similar to the type fitted to later post war open toppers. Later in the decade the workshops produced first closed top double decker. No 22 (HC 2095) pictured here decorated for the annual carnival was a 38 seater Leyland new in 1920. Towards the end of its working life it

27. From a fading sepia print, this view was taken while on layover at the Redoubt with the driver posed against the bulk of Leyland War Subsidy No 33 (HC1153).

received a Corporation body transferred from the last of the Leyland B types. After final withdrawal in 1931 the chassis was used as a lorry in the London area.

28. In the 1920s everyone seemed to be a Chaplin lookalike. Participation in the Eastbourne carnival was a regular event. In this case involving No 22 (HC2095).

In the 1920s the Corporation's transport department was active in building replacement bodies for its bus fleet. The extended garage which had served as a

munitions factory during the war was well equipped. The vehicle shown here in the early 20s is based on a Leyland 30/36 chassis new in 1919 but again the body originates from a Leyland B type of 1914 which had its chassis requisioned by the war department. In 1926 double decker No 40 was rebodied as a single decker and renumbered 36. The new body was probably built in the premises of the Eastbourne Aviation Company near St Antonys Hill which the Corporation had moved into in 1926. The Eastbourne Aviation Company had housed a RNAS training school on its airfield and had built 200 Avro aircraft during the war. However the Armistice brought financial ruin despite efforts to raise cash through operating joy rides from the seafront. In 1921 a contract to build coach

29. No 40 (HC1159) carried a body dating back to 1914 but its chassis is post war. In 1926 it received a locally built single deck body.

bodies on ex army Mc Curd lorries was cancelled at short notice when they were discovered to be wider than allowed by law. The assetts of the EAC were disposed of in 1924 and the company dissolved in 1932. Just how long HC1159 and its sister HC 1161 survived with their locally produced bodies is not recorded.

The 1924 Leylands (No 16-20) were the last vehicles of their generation to enter the fleet built to a traditional Leyland open top design subcontracted to Vickers. Around 1927/8 they were fitted with pneumatic tyres. Photographs of older vehicles in the early 1930s are rare but personal reminicences of fitters confirm the fitting of pneumatics to other buses at this time including the home produced enclosed double decker No 38. The arrival of TD3 models and the withdrawal of nos. 16-20 in 1934 saw the end of open top services until the first purpose built conversion in 1949.

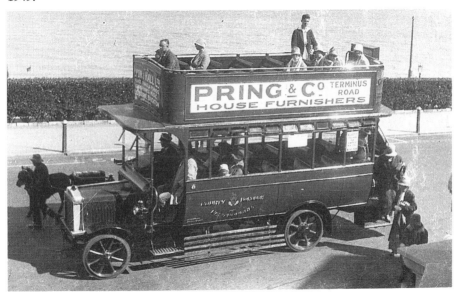

30. The Leyland buses received in 1924 were the last of the then traditional open top double deck design.

A batch of PLSC 3s purchased in 1928, seating 35, followed on from a batch of shorter PLSC 1s. By the time their withdrawal has started in 1939 they must have looked quite antiquated, two of the last batch lasted until the final year of the war. Seen at the Pier about 1935 is No 55, carrying standard fleet livery set off by black mud guards and gold lining. Destination screens in the 30s were black letters on a white background, a more usual type of screen together with a limited use of route numbers developed during the war. The photographer was D.W.K. Jones, without whose visit to the town virtually a whole decade of Corporation bus history would have passed without visual record. Withdrawn in 1941, No 55 passed to Asford Urban District Council. Others of the batch were used as water tender, ambulance and air raid precaution vehicles.

31. Two of the PLSC Lion batch new in 1928 survived in the Corporation fleet until 1945, by which time they would have looked ready for the scrap heap. Seen here at the pier in better times is No 55 (HC8637).

32. A sad episode in the history of Eastbournes buses, the General Strike did not deter these volunteer crews.

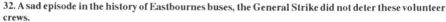

Posing for the camera in front of a Leyland single decker the conductor and driver were amongst those determined to continue the bus service during the general strike of 1926. On a bright spring morning the citizens of Eastbourne along with other towns all around the country awoke to find Tuesday 4th May a day of industrial strife. An economic depression had caused some employers, particularly in the coalfields, to cut rates of pay. Coupled with poor living conditions this created a powderkeg which exploded into the general strike. The effects were patchy with some regions almost normal and others at a standstill, in Eastbourne the transport workers were the largest group to take action. In the capital, parliament passed emergency legislation and in Eastbourne an emergency committee was formed.

The station was deserted except for a few curious onlookers while others gathered around radio sets awaiting news of the strike, the rumours of possible shortages in food and fuel far exceeded the reality. Queues formed at the Town Hall as the call went out for volunteers. Like the railmen, the bus crews ceased working on the Monday night with Corporation and Southdown men joining the 3000 strikers in the town. Expecting civil unrest, special constables along with extra firecrews were sworn in and guards posted on the bus garages. Amongst the first volunteers the local coach firms provided crews and vehicles whilst the transport undertakings used indoor staff and management to best advantage. A few non-union men continued to work and during the first morning Southdown managed to operate to Willington, Polegate and Hailsham. By the afternoon, in conjunction with Maidstone and District, services extended to Herstmonceux and Hastings.

EASTBOURNE - AND THE STRIKE

EMERGENCY COMMITTEE & CORPORATION BUSMEN

33. Both Company and Corporation bus crews joined railway workers in the strike.

34. Ignored in most accounts of Eastbourne's history, the success in putting the strike behind them helped the Corporation to re-establish its family atmosphere.

THE END OF THE STRIKE

SETTLEMENT WITH THE BUSMEN

NORMAL RAILWAY SERVICE RESUMED

Notices were soon posted inviting applications for the positions vacated by the striking crews who were now legally deemed to have resigned their positions. Despite measures like this, there was little violence or abuse on the streets in Eastbourne. It must have hurt the strikers to see a comprehensive bus service operating within the town based mainly upon charabancs. Striking crews were further intimidated when posters instructed them to return their uniforms and equipment or face prosecution. Despite this only one employee asked to return and was re-instated. With an eventual settlement of the dispute in mind both parties turned to consider the conditions which would apply with a return to work. The conditions set out by the Corporation were put before a delegation of busmen on Saturday 15th May when men marched from the Trades Union club to the town hall and had an hour long meeting with council representatives after which the strikers marched in military fashion back to their headquarters and considered the terms before them. The strike had held firm on the railway where only the occasional train managed to journey between London and the coast. But on the bus front the private operator Southdown had managed to train sufficient crews to operate an almost regular service. The council had also been able to stand down the ad hoc operators and promised to retain the recently recruited crews who would have preference over the strikers if redundancies were required after the summer season.

In the circumstances of the time the council busmen found the terms acceptable and all returned to their old employment, but Southdown refused to employ any union members and out of 21 strikers 14 did not return.

Percy Ellison had managed to maintain services in the town and reach an acceptable agreement with his employees and the good relationship with the workforce was re-established. The ECMOD (Eastbourne Corporation Motor Omnibus Department) social scene continued to flourish, typical of which is this picture of triumph taken a few years before when the football team were runners up in the Eastbourne cup.

35. The Eastbourne Corporation Motor Omnibus Department represented the active social life amongst Corporation bus staff.

SUNDAY MORNING BUSES

DISCUSSION AT TOWN COUNCIL MEETING

36. Those opposed to buses on Sundays in the 1920s may look down from heaven with a wry smile as services have diminished on that day in recent years.

The mid 1920s saw the reintroduction of Sunday bus services although only on a seasonal basis, this helped to achieve record profits of £5744 during the year 1925-6. Fare levels were actually falling in many cases below those charged prior to the first world war. Vehicles were running more miles and carrying more passengers although the increasing age of the vehicles meant higher maintenance costs. Petrol was also steadily rising in price reaching 1s (5p) a gallon in 1926. A large sum was set aside for the purchase of new vehicles but the undertaking was still to contribute to the general rate. 770,290 passengers were carried in 1925, their journeys being accomplished in greater safety thanks to the spread of street lighting. There were 168 people employed within the transport department and despite the tribulations of the general strike in 1926, the manager Percy Ellison was at pains to praise the work of all during the year in his annual report.

In the autumn of 1926 the Council transport committee considered the continuation of Sunday services through the winter months with discussion about a limited service starting at 10am. The religious lobby had now swung slightly with the people requiring transport to church. There were light hearted banter on the subject with those opposed being accused of owning private cars. The matter was finally left to the discretion of Percy Ellison who could make what arrangements he thought necessary to meet the demand.

Other matters which were raised during the twenties were the regularity of services such as Devonshire Park buses which were often to be seen speeding along Devonshire Place trying to make up time. As well as punctuality readers of the local paper were putting pen to paper on the subject of smoking. The complaint was that non smokers were occupying seats reserved for the smokers and honest hard working men were deprived of a good puff of their pipes on their way home. Such arguments continued for many years.

In photo No 37 we see No 18 (HC4583) fitted with pneumatic tyres in the late 1920s, it is outshopped in its final livery. The original versions of the Leyland TD1 were similar but Eastbourne opted for the enclosed version when in 1930 it took delivery of a new generation of buses.

The Leyland Titan deliveries of 1930 appear to have been the subject of experimental versions of the blue and yellow livery, official predelivery photographs show vehicles finished in a variety of schemes and with different styles of lettering. One of the early TDs is seen in Photo 38 on the seafront with a non standard placing for the fleet name and a variation on the area painted yellow. Other views show very large fleetnames as with the styles elsewhere perhaps these were thought a little

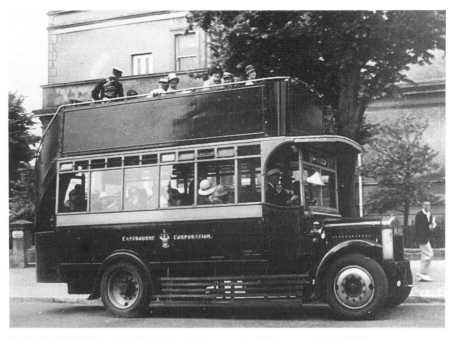

37. No 18 (HC4583) new in 1924 with solid tyres received its pneumatics in 1927.

38. The Leyland Titan deliveries of 1930 represented the latest technology in bus design and were the subject of several experimental liveries.

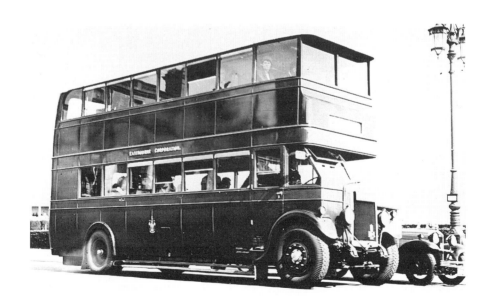

ostentatious for Eastbourne. These trials were repeated in the 1980s when a new image was sought, public opinion narrowly averted the loss of the blue from the livery although the yellow had long since been abandoned.

Corporation services during the summer seasons allowed for several routes to be supplemented during fine weather the most frequent being the parades service from the Redoubt to the Foot of Beachy Head every five minutes. The forerunner of the town tour ran along the sea front then to the station via Meads and down the Avenue to join the front again via Whitley Road. Services from the Pier to Victoria Drive and Hampden Park were also seasonal although with the withdrawal of the open top buses in the mid thirties only the seafront route remained. In the winter this service was provided by the three single deck Dennis Gs purchased in 1929.

Bad behaviour on Corporation buses was not tolerated in the 1930s. In June 1932 William Memsley of Redoubt Road who worked as a gardener in Church Street was drunk on a bus conducted by William Stubbs. The conductor did his best to quieten the merry passenger but after a tirade of abuse evicted him from the bus into the arms of the law which led to a twenty shilling (£1) fine. A penalty of double that size was handed out in 1936 after a family quarrel broke out on an Archery bound bus.

Upon the introduction of new laws covering fare collection in 1936 the local paper asked a conductor for his opinion of passengers..... "by and large the Eastbourne bus users are honest people but during the summer rush you have to keep your eyes open." Someone who didn't have his eyes open was local painter and natural historian Charles Larkin who was killed when he stepped in the path of a Corporation bus in November 1936. The transport department had a collection and sent flowers to his funeral.

Some of the problems of operating in 1936 would never be resolved. At the station passengers boarding the East Dean Road service complained that their bus was often full of passengers heading for Victoria Drive who could use the more frequent Ocklynge or Old Town services. A request for a separate stopping place was rejected due to the confined space. The changes to the routes in July 1932 which eliminated the turning of vehicles in main roads was a significant factor in improving road safety. There were now 5 minute services from Willingdon Road to Devonshire Park and 15 minute services to East Dean Road. The Hurst Arms (via Carew Road) service was extended to the pier and the St Philips Avenue service was increased to a 10 minute headway. However out of 9 services running during the summer of 1932 only the Archery - Victoria Drive and Meads service were showing a profit. Declining revenues sparked off complaints against the issue of free bus passes to councillors but scholars were to receive an additional 5% over their issue of free tickets allowing for losses. They were however severely warned against bartering these tickets.

Reduced profits were again announced in 1936 with at least £1,000 being lost on the new service to Hampden Park station. Despite this £2,500 was contributed towards

39. The distinctive doomed roof indicates its Northern Counties bodywork as No 7 (JK7428) poses in the silvern surroundings of Hampden Park.

the general rate and a record 14,343,836 passengers were carried with a total mileage of 1,384,655. The spirit of optimism was not dampened and the grand old man of Eastbourne, Percy Ellison, presented ECMOD Challenge Vase at the carnival for the best decorated pram or bike. In August of the same year he was handing out prizes again, this time to children of transport department employees who were taking part in games at the annual excursion near Pevensey Castle.

Percy Ellison had in 33 years established a fleet based upon Leyland vehicles, new deliveries reflecting developments in their products. Through the 1930s this meant a succession of petrol engined Leyland Titan double deckers which was only interrupted by the council in 1936, when the cosy relationship was shattered by competitive tendering which resulted in the delivery of handsome Strachan bodied Regent 661s. The next delivery from AEC bore the idiosyncratic body style of Northern Counties. In Picture 39 No 7 (JK7428) shows off its well rounded proportions which persisted in Northern Counties designs until the fifties. Part of a batch of five delivered in August 1938 No 7, along with its sisters, survived to become "the White Rabbit" in the Alice in Wonderland open top fleet after the war, seen in the quiet sylvan setting of Hampden Park its deep blue and yellow livery bears full lining out in gold and black and is set off by chromed fittings.

This service originated in Brodrick Road and returned to Memorial Square via Kings Drive and the Railway Station. Services to Hampden Park resumed after the first world war although they were still seasonal and terminated at the park gates off Kings Drive. By 1935 there was a regular 20 minute service to Brodrick Road from Memorial Square which was extended to Princes Park in peak season with additional journeys. The AEC fleet performed well and had completed nearly a third of a million miles each by the end of world war two.

In Picture 40, No. 5 (JK6714) stands at Langney terminus which borders the Crumbles, a unique habitat for wildlife built up by the drift of shingle along the coast. Beyond the gorse can be seen Simmonds Dairy where six decades previous Chapman had provided "leaping lessons". The Crumbles carried part of the chain of Martello towers built in the Napoleonic wars, soon tooth shaped tank traps and pill boxes would stand there.

Although not linked to the bus network until the twenties, Langney had been envisaged as a potential destination in the tramway proposal earlier in the century, when connections with the Hastings system had been put forward. The lack of railway connections ensured that buses would carry a lions share of potential custom, protective fares agreements with Southdown making Langney village corporation "territory".

At first Langney services went via Carew Road to Ocklynge or to East Dean Road but by 1935 they had settled to a 10 minute service from Langney via the station direct to Ocklynge.

40. It is hard to imagine but this quiet scene is now the location of the enlarged Langney roundabout.

41. **By the mid 1920s Southdown Motor Services Limited had established itself in Eastbourne with its offices at the Lion Brewery which would later be developed as the Southdown bus station.**

The lettering on the radiator reads "Gearless Bus" a condition achieved by a torque converter popular at the time but soon removed, delivered in August 1937 No 5 a Leyland TD5c gave twenty years of service.

Forever conservative, it was from outside the town that routes developed linking the borough with other major centres. From the west the predecessors of Southdown in particular Worthing Motor Services had extended journeys to Newhaven and Seaford and by the 1920s three buses a day traversed the downs, see Picture 41.

A Leyland SG11 chassis but with 35 seat Tilling bodywork is seen in Picture 42 at Uckfield in August 1926, it is still running on solid tyres although pneumatics would be fitted a year or so later. It was No 187 (CD9817) and although fitted with a destination box still carried a front route board. Finished in a darker shade of green than that familiar in post war years it shows to advantage the elaborate gold lining out.

Services from Uckfield to Eastbourne are first recorded on the timetable of the Tunbridge Wells operator Autocar, published in 1920 it showed a couple of journeys a day being extended to the coast but by the following year Southdown ran the Eastbourne - Uckfield service as their No 20. It was renumbered to 29 in 1922 when it provided four workings a day, a journey which took 1 hr 40 mins. In 1927 when the route became the 92 it was amended to run alternate hours either to Chailey or Golden Cross. At Uckfield connections with the mauve coloured vehicles of Autocar carried passengers northwards.

1929 was yet another year of expansion for Southdown with acquisitions which included two operators with stage carriage routes running into Eastbourne. From Hellingly came Piper's Red Saloon Motor Services running the Hellingly - Eastbourne service. In September the business of H.J. Twines Motor Services Limited was purchased along with four fairly new vehicles, two Thorneycrofts, a Dodge and a Dennis E all with single deck bus bodies. The Dennis E was only a few months old, it had a 31 seater body by Hickman and it served in the Southdown fleet in the Portsmouth area as No 392 (JK210). It was unusual for Southdown to receive acquired bus bodied vehicles, the normal intake from operators being coach types.

Twines business bought two further stage carriage routes which were the Eastbourne - Jevington route which was numbered 93 and the Eastbourne - Polegate Station service numbered 93B.

The weather over the Easter holiday in 1926 was extremely warm and encouraged visiting Londoners to enjoy Southdowns circular tours. One such party set off on the Saturday afternoon in an 18 seater Napier open charabanc fitted with pneumatic tyres. As it descended a steep hill between Friston and Jevington the driver was seized by illness and the vehicle ran off the road up a bank and overturned sending its sixteen passengers sprawling across the road. Doctors were sent for and the borough ambulance attended the scene with the injured being sent to the Princess

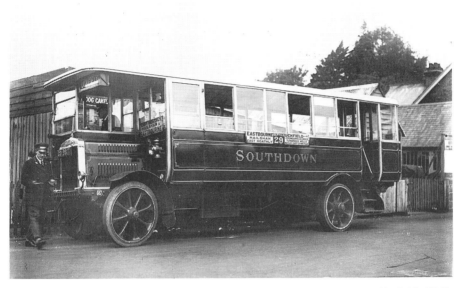

42. The first recorded bus service from Uckfield to Eastbourne was run by Autocar of Tunbridge Wells but this was soon transferred to Southdown.

43. Leyland Titan TD1 No 860 in the Southdown fleet is seen at Uckfield on the hourly service 92 to Eastbourne.

Alice Hospital in Eastbourne. The driver was still unconscious; he was Herbert Hardwick the former driver of the London to Eastbourne mailcoach and had twenty years experience driving all over the country. He soon recovered and the injured were allowed to return to their lodgings around the town.

Accidents on the roads were becoming commonplace, particularly as the number of vehicles increased and the fitting of pneumatic tyres enabled higher speeds. Such became the problem that local MP Charles Taylor would later speak in Parliament of the "carnage on the roads."

The Leyland Titan TD1 represented a radical new approach to bus design in the U.K. which was quickly taken up by operators nationwide including Eastbourne Corporation when the standard Leyland bodied full height version became available. Southdown's deliveries included early open top versions, its first enclosed bodies were delivered in 1929. The vehicle shown in Picture 43 No 860 dates from 1930, seating 48 and one of a batch of 23. The livery is lined out with dark green and gold and the bus is equipped with side destination boards, a feature which vanished before the war. It was photographed standing at Uckfield bus station on the hourly service 92 to Eastbourne. Next to the Titan stands car No 105 (BUF205), Leyland Titan TD4 of 1935, its lowbridge body would be rebuilt by West-Nor in 1947. Service 119 was half hourly, originating from Brighton with connections at Tunbridge Wells for Maidstone. It was run jointly with Maidstone & District.

As part of the BAT group, Southdown was in a good position to deal with the bureaucracy brought about by the Road Traffic Act of 1930. Already some of Eastbourne's independent tour operators had sold out to Southdown, Cavendish Coach & Car Co. in 1925, S. Foard in 26. The big combines could obtain the licences required for nationwide operations through their network of offices, but for locally based operators such as Chapmans, its extensive network of services required administration beyond its capacity. This situation was seen as an affront to the principles upon which the business had been built. The traffic commissioners could regulate routes and vehicles on private hire work in addition to regulation of excursions and stage carriage routes, its officers would monitor vehicle maintenance and could deliver hefty penalties. What was perhaps the final straw for the patience of the Chapman family was the decision by the local commissioner to award the long held excursion licence from Eastbourne to the Top of Beachy Head to Southdown. George Chapman and his brother decided that their capital invested in the business would quickly devalue unless action was taken. Southdown made the company an offer for the coach fleet, spares, goodwill and leasehold properties. A resolution recommending its acceptance was passed by a shareholders meeting, thus the Chapmans fleet passed to Southdown.

Facilities for visiting coach passengers were greatly improved when the old charabanc station in Ashford Road gained elegant buildings in the style used by the Southern Railway and was now known as the Motor Coach Station. But not all coach operators in Eastbourne thought 1932 a year of progress. After the collapse of Chapmans came the sale of Southern Glideway Coaches Limited on 5th May

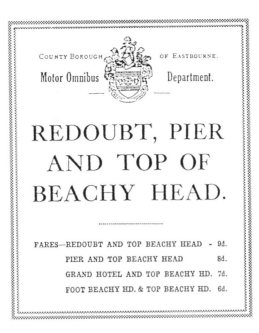

COUNTY BOROUGH OF EASTBOURNE.

Motor Omnibus Department.

REDOUBT, PIER
AND TOP OF
BEACHY HEAD.

FARES—REDOUBT AND TOP BEACHY HEAD - 9d.

PIER AND TOP BEACHY HEAD 8d.

GRAND HOTEL AND TOP BEACHY HD. 7d.

FOOT BEACHY HD. & TOP BEACHY HD. 6d.

44. It would be many years before Eastbourne municipal buses were licensed to the Top of Beachy Head but a compromise arrangement was reached for a short time in the 1930s which gave Southdown and the Corporation alternate fortnights running on the route.

45. Maidstone & District Motor Services ran into Eastbourne from the North and East, in this case on a joint service with Southdown to Hastings.

although their Managing Director Edward Southall was able to assure that all employees would be found positions with Southdown.

Operating under the regime of the new road traffic act could make life very uncomfortable for smaller concerns such as Barrow who operated in the Alfriston area. He had regular contracts with a local band to transport them to their venues. The band organiser in turn was selling tickets for these trips, the unfortunate Barrow was hauled before the traffic commissioner and found to be guilty of operating an unlicensed stage carriage service.

Although Southdown and the Corporation generally operated in harmony the relationship was sorely tested after Southdown's award of the Chapman route to the Top of Beachy Head and subsequent appeals by the Corporation against the decision. Each time the commissioners met they found in favour of Southdown although at the height of "the battle for Beachy Head" a compromise solution was to let each operator run the service alternate fortnights, hence this advertisement for the Corporation service. (See Picture 44)

Rivalry between company and Corporation also became apparent when the commissioners granted Southdown a temporary licence to operate between Hampden Park station and the nearby Sussex Agricultural Showground, the Corporation undertaking complaining that they were not even consulted on the matter. It was the spread of the town out towards Willingdon and Hampden Park which constantly tested the agreed operating areas, with the corporation regularly objecting to fare increases for Southdown journeys around the borough boundaries. The council certainly held the trump cards when allocating facilities within the town and decided that the bus stops around the station were too congested. Southdown buses had since their arrival used the stops outside and opposite the station but in 1931 they were resited up the road by the post office. This, Southdown protested, inconvenienced their customers and lost business from travellers arriving by train. Passengers bound for Corporation services towards Old Town and Ocklynge could usually shelter under the awnings of the shops but on the station side they were open to the elements. In September 1932 an agreement was reached with the Southern Railway for the provision of a canopy for bus passengers.

In 1932 an Eastbourne based Southdown driver was exonerated from blame after being involved in a fatal accident at Horsebridge in which two motorcyclists from London were killed. Passengers testified to the desperate efforts of the Southdown driver to avoid the collision. Another incident involving a motorcycle happened in 1934 when a cyclist was killed in Beach Road. The 1930s were a bad period for Southdown accidents, three Eastbourne residents were killed when their car collided with one of the company's buses on the Plumpton-Ditchling Road.

The first Maidstone & District vehicle to reach Eastbourne arrived in June 1919 with one bus outstationed at the brewery yard at what was to become the Pevensey Road bus station. At this stage routes were lettered and it was service O (which became 15) which was the first, followed by what became the 26 to Pevensey Bay via Westham. By June 1920 the 15 was joint with Southdown. It seems likely that the 26 was a joint operation but passed to Southdown by May 1924. At first the 26 ran via Hide Hollow but was amended to run via Stone Cross and shortly after renumbering to 96 in 1927 it was a circular returning via Pevensey Bay Road.

The Harrington bodied Leyland Tiger provided the usual coach design for Maidstone and District in the 1930s but far more exotic was Thorneycroft Cygnet No 850 (KJ6981) Picture 45 with 32 seater Strachan and Brown bodywork. It had been delivered new in 1932 to Weald of Kent Transport Co. of Tenterden but just over a year later the business was taken over by M & D. No 850 was transferred to the Hastings area and is seen working the joint Southdown/M & D service 99 running between Hastings and Eastbourne via Bexhill, Pevensey and Pevensey Bay.

It retains some prewar features such as the route board but lacks the elaborate lining out of earlier years. The dark green livery showed the elegant scrolled fleetname to the best advantage with the lighter areas painted cream. It was a functional yet attractive livery but lacked that special sparkle of Southdown green which so well reflected the colours of the Downs.

46. Eastbourne No 57 with a fresh coat of paint on the roof, had recently returned from service with Lancashire United.

4. WAR TIME AUSTERITY

Then Tops off along the Seafront

Eastbourne Corporation entered the war with a bus fleet of 55 vehicles, which during the hostilities was reduced by withdrawals, damage and requisitioning. Eastbourne was immediately declared a closed area and much of its population evacuated leaving at its lowest just 15% of the normal inhabitants. All this must have come as a shock to J. Atherton who had only just been appointed General Manager, arriving in 1939 from Leigh in Lancashire. The whole fleet was detailed as an army transport reserve and contracts were placed which led to the carriage of over 80,000 men engaged on coastal defence construction. Buses were frequently required to assist with rail replacement services but for all the extra passengers carried and war work undertaken the fleet was reduced as buses went to serve with air raid precautions, the National Fire Service, as water tenders, Womens Voluntary Service canteens, Royal Navy training schools and with the army. 50% of the workforce left to join the services, all survived to return but their colleagues at home suffered three fatalities. There were two direct hits on the Churchdale Road depot and frequent damage from enemy aircraft using their last bombs as they crossed the coast back to occupied France. Three buses were hit in service but their chassis survived, two were rebodied and a third, an AEC Regent with Strachan body, was converted to a breakdown tender. This survived for many years and was affectionately known as *Monty*, recalling one of Britains best known wartime generals.

In Picture 46 No 83 (JK3722) a TD3c of 1934 is seen as returned from service with Lancashire United, still showing its temporary fleet number E83. A start on freshening up its appearance includes a partially painted roof. War time features include white mudguard and life preservers. The fleet name has been obliterated but patch painting with available supplies has enabled revenue from cinema advertising on a pale blue or grey background. The Classic cinema remained a legacy of more leisurely days; until the sixties tea was dispensed in the interval from an urn borne by the usherette.

The interior view in Picture 47 was taken in one of the 1938 AEC Regents and shows the elaborate blackout arrangements which were fitted to prevent observation by enemy aircraft. To assist the conductor faced with minimal light and crowded buses passengers are requested to tender exact fares but happier days are recalled with the advertisement for the refreshment pavilion at Hampden Park.

The long years of the second world war are over and Eastbourne Corporation No 86 (JK 3725), the last of the 1934 batch of Leyland TD3s, stands behind AEC Regent No8 (JK7429) four years its junior. Picture 48 clearly demonstrates the process of returning the fleet to normal although No 86 had a few years left to serve as it was withdrawn in 1950 and dismantled for spares. Unlike sister vehicles which had been loaned to Lacashire United and Southdown, No 86 remained in Eastbourne throughout the hostilities and still carries the grey paint which covered the white

47. Interior view of a 1938 Northern Counties bodied AEC Regent shows the wartime black out arrangements.

48. No 8 in its post war livery contrasts with No 86 which, still in grey paint, was typical of the condition of vehicles emerging from over five years of frontline service on the homefront.

49. Leyland Titan No 72, which dated back to 1931, would receive a repaint but withdrawal in January 1948 was not far away.

50. The conductor of No 88 is changing the clock at the bus stop which indicates the time of the next departure. With buses on a 3 or 4 minute headway on some routes it seems superfluous.

roof and yellow panels. The prewar Tamplins advertisements have survived and contrast with plainer style on No 8. The fleet number was black on a white square to stand out on the dull background. During the war the fleetname had been obliterated to confuse any enemy paratroopers landing on the coast.

Standing proudly in its post war livery, Regent No8 would not leave the fleet until 1962 after a period as open top "White Lady".

In picture 49 remnants of pre-war lined livery survive amidst the patch painting on Leyland Titan No 72 of 1931 vintage. Although withdrawn in January 1948 it probably received a repaint. The white life preservers and mud guards again recall the war time blackout. Inside, black curtains would be drawn during hours of darkness and masked headlamps would have provided little illumination. Road traffic accidents soared during the war despite the lack of private cars. The route number was a rarity and the vehicle is given an unbalanced appearance by the oddly placed fleetname.

Just as the Leyland Titan TD1 was distinguished from the corporations TD2s by the larger destination screen on the latter, so the TD3cs could be told from the later model TD4cs of 1935.

In Picture 50 the driver of No 88 (JK6062) waits while the conductor changes the clock to show the time of the next departure. This view taken at the same time as that of No 85 (which stands behind No 88) encapsulates the atmosphere of austerity Eastbourne with both railway station and Gildredge Hotel showing signs of bomb damage and the roads pitted and uneven. No 88 a TD4c of 1935 was to be withdrawn in July 1951. The bus is heading for Upper Willingdon, it originated from Friday Street near Stone Cross, a route made possible by the 1937 extension of the borough act.

By the end of 1949 the vehicle policy for the next decade was evident, continued withdrawal of pre-war vehicles with selected conversions to open top and further deliveries of new double deckers from the two rivals, AEC and Leyland. Bodywork would be supplied by East Lancs and their subsidiary, Bruce Coach works. However there are always exceptions to any rule and the largest batch of buses since the TD1s of the early thirties were eight Crossleys. A feature of the Corporation's fleet at this time was the absence of two seats in the centre of the lower saloon which enabled easier circulation for the conductor which was a particular problem with the short distance between town centre stops and the heavy loadings.

One of the 1946 Leyland PD1s No 13 (JK9111) which would later be converted to open top in Picture 51 is standing in front of the bomb site on which the present Marks & Spencer and post office were built. No 13 is bound for Langney on what would become route 1. The 10 minute frequency was enhanced by vehicles working the Friday Street - Upper Willindgdon route and from Langney to Cherry Gardens, both hourly. The Archery - Station section was also covered by Ocklynge and

51. New in 1946, No 13 a Leyland PD1 stands in front of the bomb site on which Marks & Spencer and the Post Office would be built.

52. Post War shortages have delayed repair to the rear window of No 17 (JK9115) a typical bus of Eastbourne's new fleet with characteristic East Lancs bodywork.

53. AEC Regal No 11 (AHC411) was purchased for use on contract work but throughout its life saw peak hour duties on regular services.

54. No 64 had an eventful life. After a direct hit in the war it was rebodied and, as shown here on service to Hampden Park, ran as an open topper until 1956. It has recently rejoined the fleet.

Hampden Park buses which gave an interval of 3 minutes between buses, often less at peak times.

No 17 (JK9115) typifies the Eastbourne post war standard being a Leyland Titan PD1 (see Picture 52). New in 1947, post war shortages have obviously delayed repair of the damaged platform window in this view taken around 1951. No 17 stands at Dukes Drive at the top of the parades ready to make the return journey from the Foot of Beachy Head. The "parades" route later numbered 6 was usually augmented in the summer season by additional buses, which with the re-introduction of open-toppers attracted plenty of business from holiday makers. A variety of extended routes taking in all or part of the seafront were also regular seasonal features. In 1947 an hours return ride would cost 1s (5p). Boarding No 17 for its destination at Princes Park would cost 4d(2p). No 17 itself became an open topper in 1963, serving for 5 years in this guise. It carried advertisements for route eight and was thus a regular on seasonal services to Hampden Park.

The postwar fleet had only one single decker at its disposal for contract work, as colleges re-opened and new schools were built on the perimeters of the borough a sister vehicle for Leyland Lion No 12 was required. This duly arrived in the form of AEC Regal III (AHC 411) which was numbered eleven. Its dual bus/coach body seated 30 supplied by the usual bodybuilder for the fleet at the time, East Lancs. Finish was in the normal blue and yellow livery but without black lining. It later received a livery of broken white relieved with blue and in 1970 was renumbered 93, making space in the numbering sequence for a new Atlantean. Both Lion and Regal assisted in normal traffic duties at peak times. In Picture 53, taken in Seaside Road approaching the junction with Terminus Road, the Regal in its original livery is bound for Ocklynge. Bus stops around Barkers corner were always busy; No 13 (JK9111) has already picked up more passengers for Langney. Langney Road was still a focal point for shopping and was near the main cinemas.

The post war years saw a boom in British seaside holidays bringing plenty of visitors to Eastbourne. Although the municipal buses lacked the licence to run to Beachy Head they still found ample passengers wanting to take in the sea air and obtain fine view of the channel from an open top bus. During the summer of 1949 a fifteen year old Leyland Titan, No 80 was converted in the corporation workshop, the first of ten Titans to be given such a new lease of life. The early Titans were in turn replaced in the mid fifties when an entire batch of AEC regents dating from 1939 received the open top treatment. Open top Titan TD4s and 5s were replaced by Leyland PD1s in the early sixties. In Picture 54 Leyland Titan TD1 No 64 is bound for Hampden Park about 1952. The livery is unrelieved broken white with blue wheels. This particular vehicle had already been rebodied by East Lancs in 1944 after destruction during a Luftwaffe attack.

In Picture 55 the exhuberence of the schoolboys exemplifies the spirit which was about to end the austerity days of post war Britain. Terminus Road still appears spacious if a bit uneven and in the background the Post Office and Louis G Ford stand on the site of the original railway station. Just to prove that even the "sun

55. An austere scene in Terminus Road as Crossley No 34 (JK9991) approaches the main bus stops which were located outside the railway station.

56. Southdown No 160 (EUF160) typifies the Company at war; the usual high standards are retained and even a coat of utility grey paint cannot stop that sparkle on the bodywork.

strap of the south" has its off days, No 34 (JK9991) splashes its way into Terminus Road. One of a batch of eight Crossley DD42/5s of 1948 which stood apart from AEC Regents and Leyland PD2s of the same vintage. This nearside view was chosen to show the small destination screen above the fourth window bay, half the normal size. The Crossley radiator was a rare sight in the South but the Lancashire built body from Blackburn was usual fare for Eastbourne.

After leaving the station No 34 will head down Langney Road and Cavendish Avenue bound for the terminus at St. Philips Avenue, close to the Churchdale Road Depot. Downs Avenue replaced Ocklynge as destination for St. Philips Avenue services after the war and before numbering of routes became universal it was shown on destination blinds as 1A. By the middle sixties the service was extended a little to serve Newick Road but by then the Crossleys had been withdrawn.

The diversion of the Corporation fleet to wartime duties was relatively straight forward compared with the Southdown company which had a network of services stretching from Hampshire to Kent. What proved to be a simple but efficient means of allowing for the delays due to the black out and heavy loadings was the addition of one minute in ten to running times enabling connections to be maintained. There were cuts in services, particularly Sunday morning schedules, but the basic local network was retained. Fluctuations in the local population saw evacuees arriving from London, people being moved from coastal defence areas and influxes of defence workers. This resulted in a 50% increase in passengers carried despite the company having released over 160 vehicles at the start of the war. The company did receive new vehicles, those later in the war were to strict utility specifications which included slatted wooden seating, limited ventilation and small masked headlamps. Older vehicles such as Leyland Titan TD1s and 2s were rebodied, extending their lives although the quality of materials in the war years was such that unseasoned timber for instance soon rotted. Various attempts to reduce the visibility of buses from the air were tried, roofs were painted dark green or grey, many vehicles had total repaints, dark green below the saloon windows and everything above grey, there were doubtless many variations. All carried white edges on mudguards and headlamp masks. Trials with producer gas powered buses in Worthing and Brighton were of limited success and were unsuitable for journeys over the Downs.

Picture 56 is a rare wartime photograph of car No 160 (EUF160) a Leyland TD5 of 1938 waiting to make the return journey from East Grinstead to Eastbourne. It displays all the features of a thirties Southdown bus at war; its Park Royal lowbridge body is painted green and grey but still retains its gleam. Masked headlamps were of little help to the driver or other road users. The vehicle survived to be rebodied by Beadles in 1949 and was withdrawn in 1959. At the start of the war route 92 ran from Eastbourne to East Grinstead hourly with additional short workings which were eliminated in the war, a black out journey time of 2 hours 34 minutes was allowed. Later in the war Sunday morning journeys were withdrawn. Given Southdown's front line role, it is surprising that there were few casualties amongst staff and passengers.

57. Pevensey Road Bus Station in a very early post World War II scene is pictured with Southdown No 173 on service 96 to Pevensey Bay.

Picture 57 is a very early post war view taken inside Pevensey Road bus station. No 173 (EUF173) was delivered new in April 1939, its Park Royal lowbridge body seating 52. At quarter past the hour it would leave on service 96 for Pevensey Bay via Stone Cross. In December 1947 its body was removed to be replaced in January by an East Lancs highbridge body which lasted until 1960.

Such was the post war programme of rebuilding and rebodying that vehicles from identical batches took on totally different appearances, this vehicle No 110 was from the same batch as No 105 seen with the TD1 at Uckfield but has been rebodied by Beadle in 1947. Of the batch of ten buses no less than four companies were involved in changing their bodies. No 110 was withdrawn in 1956. In Picture 58 it is seen heading into Terminus Road, past the station on hourly route No 93. The Corporation Crossley No 37 has lost its early postwar lined livery unlike the Southdown bus which retained dark green lining but cannot match the artwork of the corporation painted advertisements.

In no way typical of Southdown double deckers in 1950 was No 700 (KUF700) which was a Leyland PD2/12 with NCME double deck coach body seating 44. It was intended for express work between Eastbourne and London and was exhibited at the 1950 commercial motor show. It was not a success and Picture 59 is a rare view of it in service passing through Croydon on its return journey.

Typical of the 1930s style of single deck bus in Picture 60 is Southdown No 1453 (FCD253) which was new in October 1938. Its bodywork was by a builder much favoured by Southdown, Harringtons of Hove. This view dating from about 1950 shows it waiting over in Elms Avenue opposite the pier, while working the 97 which was running every 15 minutes to Beachy Head. By the end of the decade though still running year round, peak frequency was 30 minutes with about 6 journeys a day out of season.

Between 1941 and 1945 No 1453 was converted to perimeter seating enabling large numbers of standing passengers to be carried at a time when private motoring was discouraged. In November 1952 it was withdrawn from service and its bodywork removed. The chassis was retained along with those from similar vehicles and used to construct a Leyland/Beadle coach with a full front body.

Other vehicles used on the 97 included two Leyland Tigers delivered in 1934, which were joined by two more in 1935. They had Short Bros. bodies which were almost to coach specifications. Their centre entrance bodies coped with the crowds travelling to the top of Beach Head while legislation prohibited the use of double deckers on the route.

During World War II the need for double deck buses was such that Southdown was allocated a hundred between 1943 and 1946. The principal war time model available was the Guy Arab, most of those supplied having 5LW engines. The Park Royal body on No 412 (GUF72) in Picture 61 would have been constructed with unseasoned timber which rotted quickly. A postwar boom in seaside holidays was

58. Rebodied by Beadle, No 110 passes Eastbourne Corporation No 37 at the railway station. No less than four companies were involved in the rebuilding of this batch of Southdown buses.

59. At the time unique and giving a foretaste of the famous PD3 Queen Mary class, this is Southdown No 700. Originally intended for the Eastbourne to London route, it was eventually relegated to contract work.

60. Harringtons of Hove provided the bodywork on Southdown No 1453 (FCD253). It is seen on layover from service 97 which ran every 15 minutes to Beachy Head.

61. From the hundred utility double deck buses allocated to Southdown in World War II were several which later saw service on seaside open top duties, in this case No 412 (FUF72).

62. One of the last 1935 vintage buses to be withdrawn was No 113 (BUF213) seen here with a new East Lancs body on a service 12 relief in Langney Road.

63. Southdown's Royal Parade garage was demolished and is now the site of a block of flats.

64. Southdown Leyland Tiger TS7 is taking a short run to the Wannock Tea Gardens. During World War II this coach had seen service as an ambulance.

THE WORLD'S FIRST MUNICIPAL MOTOR OMNIBUS SERVICE
CELEBRATING 90 YEARS OF SERVICE TO EASTBOURNE 1903 - 1993

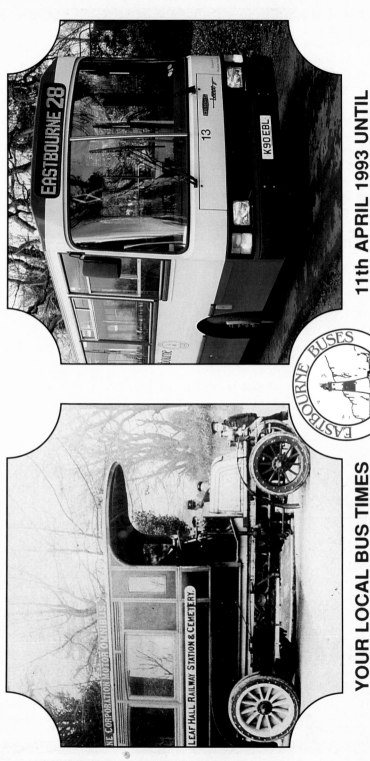

11th APRIL 1993 UNTIL 2nd OCTOBER 1993

EASTBOURNE BUSES 1903 ~ 1993

YOUR LOCAL BUS TIMES
Bus Enquiries Tel: (0323) 416416

Services 13/13A

HAMPDEN PARK—LANGNEY—CRUMBLES—TOWN CENTRE—OCKLYNGE—GENERAL HOSPITAL—HAMPDEN PARK

(Via Brassey Avenue, Lottbridge Drove, Willingdon Drove, The Rising, Priory Road, Marsden Farm Estate, Pevensey Bay Road, Ramsay Way, Lottbridge Drove, Seaside, Upperton Road, Rodmill Drive, Kings Drive, Lindfield Road, Maywood Avenue)

13 – CLOCKWISE CIRCULAR SERVICE   13A – ANTI-CLOCKWISE CIRCULAR SERVICE

Mondays to Saturdays

Service No. 13

	X					Then at these minutes past each hour						UNTIL				
Maywood Ave. (Magnolia Walk)	–	–	0758	0828	0858	28	58	1658	1728	1758	–	2017	2117	2217
Hampden Park Station ⇌	–	–	0802	0832	0902	32	02	1702	1732	1802	–	2020	2120	2220
Langney (Shopping Centre)	0630	0710	0737	0807	0907	37	07	1707	1737	1807	1925	2025	2125	2225
Crumbles Centre (Asda)	–	0720	0747	0817	0847	0917	47	17	1717	1747	1817	1933	2033	2133	2233
Ramsay Way	0638	0722	0749	0819	0849	0919	49	19	1719	1749	1819	1935	2035	2135	2235
Sovereign Centre	0641	0725	0752	0822	0852	0922	52	22	1722	1752	1822	1937	2037	2137	2237
Seaside (Alexandra Arms)	0643	0727	0754	0824	0854	0924	54	24	1724	1754	1824	1939	2039	2139	2239
Terminus Road ⇌ arr.	0655	0739	0806	0836	0906	0936	06	36	1736	1806	1836	1948	2048	2148	2248
Terminus Road ⇌ dep.	–	0740	0810	0840	0910	0940	10	40	1740	–	–	1958	2058	2158	2258
Kings Drive (General Hospital)	–	0750	0820	0850	0920	0950	20	50	1750	–	–	2008	2108	2208	2308
Maywood Ave. (Magnolia Walk)	–	0756	0826	0856	0926	0956	26	56	1756	–	–	2014	2114	2214	2314
														★

Service No. 13A

	MF★	★			Then at these minutes past each hour							UNTIL							
Maywood Ave. (Magnolia Walk)	0746	0816	0846	0916	46	16	1646	1716	1746	1857	1957	2057	2157	2244
Kings Drive (General Hospital)	0752	0822	0852	0922	52	22	1652	1722	1752	1903	2003	2103	2203	2250
Terminus Road ⇌ arr.	0802	0832	0902	0932	02	32	1702	1732	1802	1913	2013	2113	2213	2300
Terminus Road ⇌ dep.	0808	0838	0908	0938	08	38	1708	1738	1805	1923	2023	2123	2213	2303
Seaside (Arlington Arms)	0819	0849	0919	0949	19	49	1719	1749	1814	1934	2034	2134	2224	2314
Sovereign Centre	0821	0851	0921	0951	21	51	1721	1751	1816	1936	2036	2136	2226	2316
Ramsay Way	0824	0854	0924	0954	24	54	1724	1754	1819	1938	2038	2138	2228	2318
Crumbles Centre (opp. Asda)	0826	0856	0926	0956	26	56	1726	1756	1821	1946	2046	2146	2236	2328
Langney (Shopping Centre)	0836	0906	0936	1006	36	06	1736	1806	1831	1946	2046	2146	2236	2328
Hampden Park Station ⇌	0841	0911	0941	1011	41	11	1741	–	–	1951	2051	2151	2241	–
Maywood Ave. (Magnolia Walk)	0844	0914	0944	1014	44	14	1744	–	–	1954	2054	2154	2244	–

Sundays

Service No. 13

			Then at these minutes past each hour	UNTIL	
Maywood Ave. (Magnolia Walk)	–	–	17	–	2217
Hampden Park Station ⇌	–	–	20	–	2220
Langney (Shopping Centre)	1025		25		2225
Crumbles Centre (Asda)	1033		33		2233
Ramsay Way	1035		35		2235
Sovereign Centre	1037		37		2237
Seaside (Alexandra Arms)	1039		39		2239
Terminus Road ⇌ arr.	1048		48		2248
Terminus Road ⇌ dep.	1058		58		2258
Kings Drive (General Hospital)	1108		08		2308
Maywood Ave. (Magnolia Walk)	1114		14		2314
					★

Service No. 13A

			Then at these minutes past each hour	UNTIL		
Maywood Ave. (Magnolia Walk)	0957	1057	57		2157	2244
Kings Drive (General Hospital)	1003	1103	03		2203	2250
Terminus Road ⇌ arr.	1013	1113	13		2213	2300
Terminus Road ⇌ dep.	1023	1123	23		2213	2303
Seaside (Arlington Arms)	1032	1132	32		2222	2312
Sovereign Centre	1034	1134	34		2224	2314
Ramsay Way	1036	1136	36		2226	2316
Crumbles Centre (opp. Asda)	1038	1138	38		2228	2318
Langney (Shopping Centre)	1046	1146	46		2236	2326
Hampden Park Station ⇌	1051	1151	51		2241	–
Maywood Ave. (Magnolia Walk)	1054	1154	54		2244	–

X – Journey on Service 1 on Mondays to Fridays.   ★ – Operates to or from Hampden Park Station.   This Service passes near the MGM Cinema at Crumbles Centre.

MF – Operates on Mondays to Fridays.   For additional buses serving Ramsay Way and Crumbles Centre see Services 26/28.   ⇌ – Near to British Rail Station.

Services 12/12A WILLINGDON TREES—WINKNEY FARM—BIRCH ROAD—TOWN CENTRE—OLD TOWN—HOSPITAL—WILLINGDON TREES

(Via Hazelwood Avenue, Lottbridge Drove, Seaside, Upperton Road, The Goffs, High Street, Church Street, Green Street, Victoria Drive, Eldon Road, Rodmill Drive, Kings Drive, Willingdon Park Drive, Hazelwood Avenue)

12 – CLOCKWISE CIRCULAR SERVICE   12A – ANTI-CLOCKWISE CIRCULAR SERVICE

Mondays to Saturdays

Service No. 12

	MF	MF	MF	S	MF	S		Then at these minutes past each hour							
Willingdon Trees (Hazelwood Ave.)	–	–	0642	–	0712	–	0742	12 42	1742	1810	1840	1940	2040	2140	2240	–
Hampden Park Station ⇌	–	–	0647	–	0717	–	0747	17 47	1747	1815	1845	1945	2045	2145	2245	–
Winkney Farm (Wilton Avenue)	–	–	0653	–	0723	–	0753	23 53	1753	1821	1851	1951	2051	2151	2251	–
The Hydneye (Cade Street)	–	–	0654	–	0724	–	0754	24 54	1754	1822	1852	1952	2052	2152	2252	–
Birch Road (Bus Garage)	0559	0629	0659	0659	0729	0729	0759	29 59	1759	1827	1857	1957	2057	2157	2257	–
Seaside (Alexandra Arms)	0601	0631	0701	0701	0731	0731	0801	31 01	1801	–	1859	1959	2059	2159	STOP	–
Terminus Road ⇌ arr.	0613	0643	0713	0713	0743	0743	0813	43 13	1813	–	1908	2008	2108	2208	–	–
Terminus Road ⇌ dep.	0617	0647	0717	0717	0747	0747	0817	47 17	1817	–	1915	2015	2115	2215	2245	–
Kings Drive (General Hospital)	0631	0701	0731	0731	0801	0801	0831	01 31	1831	–	1928	2028	2128	2228	2258	–
Willingdon Trees (Hazelwood Ave.)	0640	0710	0740	0740	0810	0810	0840	10 40	1840	–	1936	2036	2136	2236	2306 ★	–

(U N T L — "UNTIL" — marked against The Hydneye / Birch Road / Seaside / Terminus Road rows)

Service No. 12A

	MF	MF		S	Then at these minutes past each hour						
Willingdon Trees (Hazelwood Ave.)	–	–	–	0647	17 47	1817	1847	1917	2012	2112	2212
Kings Drive (General Hospital)	–	–	–	0657	27 57	1827	1857	1927	2020	2120	2220
Terminus Road ⇌ arr.	–	–	–	0712	42 12	1842	1912	1942	2033	2133	2233
Terminus Road ⇌ dep.	–	–	–	0718	48 18	1848	1912	1943	2043	2143	–
Seaside (Arlington Arms)	–	–	–	0729	59 29	1859	1921	1952	2052	2152	–
Birch Road (Bus Garage)	0601	0631	0701	0731	01 31	1901	1923	1954	2054	2154	–
Winkney Farm (Wilton Avenue)	0606	0636	0706	0736	06 36	1906	–	1959	2059	2159	–
The Hydneye (Cade Street)	0607	0637	0707	0737	07 37	1907	–	2000	2100	2200	–
Hampden Park Station ⇌	0609	0639	0709	0739	09 39	1909	–	2002	2102	2202	–
Willingdon Trees (Hazelwood Ave.)	0615	0645	0715	0745	15 45	1915	–	2008	2108	2208	–

(U N T L — "UNTIL" — marked against The Hydneye / Birch Road / Seaside / Terminus Road rows)

Sundays

Service 12

			Then at these minutes past each hour		
Willingdon Trees (Hazelwood Ave.)	–	1040	40	2240	–
Hampden Park Station ⇌	–	1045	45	2245	–
Winkney Farm (Wilton Avenue)	0951	1051	51	2251	–
The Hydneye (Cade Street)	0952	1052	52	2252	–
Birch Road (Bus Garage)	0957	1057	57	2257	–
Seaside (Alexandra Arms)	0959	1059	59	–	–
Terminus Road ⇌ arr.	1008	1108	08	–	–
Terminus Road ⇌ dep.	1015	1115	15	–	2245
Kings Drive (General Hospital)	1028	1128	28	–	2258
Willingdon Trees (Hazelwood Ave.)	1036	1136	36	–	2306 ★

(U N T L — "UNTIL" — marked against The Hydneye / Birch Road / Seaside / Terminus Road rows)

Service 12A

			Then at these minutes past each hour		
Willingdon Trees (Hazelwood Ave.)	–	1012	12	2112	2212
Kings Drive (General Hospital)	–	1020	20	2120	2220
Terminus Road ⇌ arr.	–	1033	33	2133	2233
Terminus Road ⇌ dep.	–	1043	43	2143	–
Seaside (Arlington Arms)	–	1052	52	2152	–
Birch Road (Bus Garage)	0958	1054	54	2154	–
Winkney Farm (Wilton Avenue)	1003	1059	59	2159	–
The Hydneye (Cade Street)	1004	1100	00	2200	–
Hampden Park Station ⇌	1006	1102	02	2202	–
Willingdon Trees (Hazelwood Ave.)	1012	1108	08	2208	–

(U N T L — "UNTIL" — marked against the Terminus Road / Seaside / Birch rows)

MF – Mondays to Fridays.   S – Additional journey on Saturdays.
For additional buses serving The Hydneye and Hampden Park Station see Services 11/11A.

⇌ – Near to British Rail Station.
★ – To Hampden Park Station.

Service 27 EASTBOURNE—PEVENSEY BAY—BEXHILL—HASTINGS—RYE—NEW ROMNEY (Via Sea Front, Princes Road, A259)

Sundays & Bank Hols only ★

Eastbourne (Terminus Road) ⇌	1015	1315
The Pier	1020	1320
Sovereign Centre	1026	1326
Crumbles Centre (opp. Asda)	1029	1329
Pevensey Bay (Midland Bank)	1033	1333
Pevensey (Bridge End for Castle)	1035	1335
Little Common (Roundabout)	1045	1345
Bexhill (Town Hall Square) ⇌	1051	1351
St. Leonards (Warrior Square) ⇌	1106	1406
Hastings (opp. Pier)	1111	1411
Ore (Christ Church)	1123	1423
Guestling (White Hart)	1126	1426
Winchelsea (Main Road)	1141	1441
Rye (Rail Station) ⇌	1148	1448
Appledore (Rail Station) ⇌	1159	1459
Brenzett (Cross Roads)	1206	1506
New Romney (RH & DR Station)	1216	1516

⇌ Near to British Rail Station.   ★ This journey will await connections off Services 1, 10 and 13A.

Sundays & Bank Hols only

New Romney (RH & DR Station) ⇌	1300	1600
Brenzett (Cross Roads)	1314	1614
Appledore (Rail Station) ⇌	1321	1621
Rye (Rail Station) ⇌	1332	1632
Winchelsea (Main Road)	1339	1639
Guestling (White Hart)	1354	1654
Ore (Christ Church)	1357	1657
Hastings (Pier)	1409	1709
St. Leonards (Warrior Square) ⇌	1414	1714
Bexhill (Town Hall Square) ⇌	1429	1729
Little Common (Roundabout)	1435	1735
Pevensey (Bridge End for Castle)	1445	1745
Pevensey Bay (St. Wilfrids)	1447	1747
Crumbles Centre (Asda)	1451	1751
Sovereign Centre	1454	1754
The Pier	1500	1800
Eastbourne (Terminus Road) ⇌	1505	1805

Use SERVICE 27 to visit

the

ROMNEY, HYTHE & DYMCHURCH RAILWAY

The world's smallest main-line railway with steam trains

Local Rider Services 50 60

50 LANGNEY—OLD TOWN—TOWN CENTRE
(Via Langney Rise, Shinewater, Willingdon Drove, Decoy Drive, Kings Drive, Rodmill Drive, Eldon Road)

60 LANGNEY POINT—KINGS DRIVE
(Via Princes Road, Lottbridge Drove, Seaside, Whitley Road, Kings Drive)

Schooldays only Service No.	50	60	60
Langney Roundabout	0805	0810	
Langney (Shopping Centre) ⇌	0810	—	0810
Hampden Park Station ⇌	0822	—	
Kings Drive (General Hospital)	0826	—	
Terminus Road ⇌	0840	—	
Fire Station	—	0824	
Kings Drive (Park Avenue)	—	0830	

Schooldays only Service No.	60
Kings Drive (Park Avenue)	1545
Fire Station	1551
Langney Roundabout	1606
Langney (Shopping Centre) ⇌	1610

Local Rider Service

319 HOOE—BEXHILL
(Via Whydown, Sidley)

Tuesdays & Thursdays only

Hooe (Red Lion)	*1029	1310
Whydown	1033	1305
Sidley (Sussex Hotel)	1039	1300
Bexhill (Marina)	1050	1247

⇌ — Near to British Rail Station.   Local Rider Services are operated for County Engineer, East Sussex County Council, Lewes BN7 1UE. ☎ 0273 478007.

Services 26 / 28

EASTBOURNE—PEVENSEY BAY—BEACHLANDS
(Via Seafront, Langney Point, Pevensey Bay Road, Coast Road)

EASTBOURNE—PEVENSEY BAY—BEXHILL—BATTLE—RYE
(Via Seafront, Langney Point, Pevensey Bay Road, A259, London Road, A269, Cripps Corner, A268)
Including Sunday journeys on Service 27

Mondays to Fridays

Service No.	28	28	28	26	28	26	28	26	28	28 A	26
Eastbourne (Terminus Road) ✦	0725	–	0925	1025	1125	1225	1325	1425	1525	1625	–
The Pier	0731	–	0931	1031	1131	1231	1331	1431	1531	1631	1711
Sovereign Centre	0738	–	0938	1038	1138	1238	1338	1438	1538	1638	1718
Ramsay Way	0741	–	0941	1041	1141	1241	1341	1441	1541	1641	1721
Crumbles Centre (opp. Asda)	0743	–	0943	1043	1143	1243	1343	1443	1543	1643	1723
Pevensey Bay (Midland Bank)	0747	–	0947	1047	1147	1247	1347	1447	1547	1647	1727
Beachlands (Marine Avenue)	–	–	–	1051	–	1251	–	1451	–	–	1731
Pevensey (Bridge End) ✦	0749	–	0949	–	1149	–	1349	–	1549	1649	–
Little Common (Roundabout)	0802	–	1002	–	1202	–	1402	–	1602	1702	–
Bexhill (Town Hall Square) ✦	0809	–	1009	–	1209	–	1409	–	1609	1709	–
Sidley (Sussex Hotel)	0816	–	1016	–	1216	–	1416	–	1616	1716	–
Ninfield (The Kings Arms)	0825	–	1025	–	1225	–	1425	–	1625	1725	–
Catsfield (White Hart)	0828	–	1028	–	1228	–	1428	–	1628	1728	–
Battle (Abbey) ✦	0839	0949	1039	–	1239	–	1439	–	1639	1738	–
Sedlescombe (The Green)	–	0959	1049	–	1249	–	1449	–	1649	–	–
Staplecross (The Stores)	–	1004	1054	–	1254	–	1454	–	1654	–	–
Bodiam Castle	–	1009	1059	–	1259	–	1459	–	1659	–	–
Sandhurst (The Green)	–	1014	1104	–	1304	–	1504	–	1704	–	–
Northiam (K & ESR Station)	–	1019	1109	–	1309	–	1509	–	1709	–	–
Beckley (Rose & Crown)	–	★	1115	–	1315	–	1515	–	1715	–	–
Peasmarsh (Post Office)	–	–	1124	–	1324	–	1524	–	1724	–	–
Rye (Rail Station) ✦	–	–	1134	–	1334	–	1534	–	1734	–	–

Saturdays

Service No.	28 BR	28	26	28	26	28	26	28	26	28 LR
Eastbourne (Terminus Road) ✦	–	0925	1025	1125	1225	1325	1425	1525	1625	1705
The Pier	–	0931	1031	1131	1231	1331	1431	1531	1631	1711
Sovereign Centre	–	0938	1038	1138	1238	1338	1438	1538	1638	1718
Ramsay Way	–	0941	1041	1141	1241	1341	1441	1541	1641	1721
Crumbles Centre (opp. Asda)	0613	0943	1043	1143	1243	1343	1443	1543	1643	1723
Pevensey Bay (Midland Bank)	0617	0947	1047	1147	1247	1347	1447	1547	1647	1727
Beachlands (Marine Avenue)	–	–	1051	–	1251	–	1451	–	–	–
Pevensey (Bridge End) ✦	0619	0949	–	1149	–	1349	–	1549	1649	1729
Little Common (Roundabout)	0632	1002	–	1202	–	1402	–	1602	1702	–
Bexhill (Town Hall Square) ✦	0639	1009	–	1209	–	1409	–	1609	1709	–
Sidley (Sussex Hotel)	0646	1016	–	1216	–	1416	–	1616	1716	–
Ninfield (The Kings Arms)	0655	1025	–	1225	–	1425	–	1625	1725	–
Catsfield (White Hart)	0658	1028	–	1228	–	1428	–	1628	1728	–
Battle (Abbey) ✦	0709	1039	–	1239	–	1439	–	1639	–	–
Sedlescombe (The Green)	0719	1049	–	1249	–	1449	–	1649	–	–
Staplecross (The Stores)	0724	1054	–	1254	–	1454	–	1654	–	–
Bodiam Castle	0729	1059	–	1259	–	1459	–	1659	–	–
Sandhurst (The Green)	0734	1104	–	1304	–	1504	–	1704	–	–
Northiam (K & ESR Station)	0739	1109	–	1309	–	1509	–	1709	–	–
Beckley (Rose & Crown)	0745	1115	–	1315	–	1515	–	1715	–	–
Peasmarsh (Post Office)	0754	1124	–	1324	–	1524	–	1724	–	–
Rye (Rail Station) ✦	0804	1134	–	1334	–	1534	–	1734	–	–

Sundays

	Service No.	27	27
Eastbourne (Terminus Road) ✦		1015	1315
The Pier		1020	1320
Sovereign Centre		1026	1326
Ramsay Way		1029	1329
Crumbles Centre (opp. Asda)		1033	1333
Pevensey Bay (Midland Bank)		1035	1335
Little Common (Roundabout)		1045	1345
Bexhill (Town Hall Square) ✦		1051	1351
Via Hastings to New Romney			
Rye (Rail Station) ✦		1148	1448

✦ – Near to British Rail Station.   A – Via Bexhill 6th Form College.   LR – Local Rider journey.
BR – Starts from Birch Road (Bus Garage) at 0611 hours.   ★ – Terminates at Goddens Gill 3 minutes later.

Service 2 LANGNEY—SHINEWATER—BIRCH ROAD—BRIDGEMERE—TOWN CENTRE—OLD TOWN—FARLAINE ROAD

(Via Milfoil Drive, Larkspur Drive, Willingdon Drove, Lottbridge Drove, Seaside, Churchdale Road, Bridgemere Road, St. Philips Avenue, Memorial Roundabout, The Goffs, High Street, Church Street, Green Street)

Mondays to Saturdays only

Langney → Town Centre → Farlaine Road

Stop	MF	MF	MF	MF	Sch	H	MF	S	MF	S	...min past hour...		MF	W/S	Sch	MF	S	MF	MF
											MF	S							
Langney (Shopping Centre)	–	–	–	–	–	0801	–	0925	–	0955	25	55	1525	1534	–	1655	–	2110	2210
Shinewater (Milfoil Drive)	–	–	–	–	–	0805	–	0929	–	0959	29	59	1529	–	–	1659	–	–	–
Birch Road (Bus Garage)	0637	0706	0725	0755	0812	CR	0906	0936	0826	1006	36	06	1536	1545	1559	1706	–	2112	2212
Seaside (Alexandra Arms)	0639	0708	0727	0757	0814	0828	0908	0938	CR	1008	38	08	1538	1548	1613	1708	–	–	–
Bridgemere Road	0642	0711	0730	0800	0817	0831	0911	0941	CR	1011	41	11	1541	1550	1615	1711 (CR)	–	2115	2215
Terminus Road ⇌ arr.	0654	0723	0742	0812	0827	0843	0923	0953	0911	1023	53	23	1553	1611 (CR)	1623	1723	–	2127	2227
Terminus Road ⇌ dep. (D)	–	0723	0742	0812	0830	0843	0923	0953	0911	1023	–	–	–	1623	1627	1730	–	2130	2230
Farlaine Road	–	–	0823	–	0841	–	–	–	–	–	–	–	–	1638	–	–	–	2140	2240

Farlaine Road → Town Centre → Langney

Stop	MF	MF	MF	MF	S	...min past hour...		W	S	Sch	MF	S	MF	MF	MF
						MF	S								
Farlaine Road	–	–	–	–	–	04	34	–	–	1531	–	1531	–	–	–
Terminus Road ⇌ arr.	–	0845	0857	–	–	–	–	1547	1559	–	1645	1657	1804	2008	2141
Terminus Road ⇌ dep.	0814	0847	0904	0904	0934	04	34	1504	1515	1548	1704	1715	1953	2018	2151
Bridgemere Road	0825	0858	0915	0915	0945	15	45	1513	1518	1610	1715	1718	2003	2020	2153
Birch Road (Bus Garage)	0828	0901	0918	0918	0948	18	48	1518	1548	1613	1718	1745	2006	2030	2203
Seaside (Arlington Arms)	0830	0903	0920	0920	0950	20	50	1520	1550	1615	1720	1748	2008	2033	2206
Bridgemere Road	–	–	–	–	–	–	–	–	1620	1650	1720	1750	2035	2206	2208
Shinewater (Milfoil Drive)	0837	–	0927	0927	0957	27	57	1527	1623	1657	1723	1818	2033	2127	2208
Langney (Shopping Centre)	0841	–	0931	0931	1001	31	01	1531	1627	1701	1750	1820	2035	2130	2303
Langney (Shopping Centre)	–	0931	–	–	–	–	–	–	–	–	–	2008	2206	2306	2315

(Late journeys continue: ... 2241 / 2251 / 2253 ... 2306 / 2308 / 2315 / 2319)

Service 3 — SEA FRONT SERVICE
SOVEREIGN CENTRE—PIER—BEACHY HEAD

Whenever possible journeys will be operated with Open-Top Buses

Daily

		NS			★		NS	NS	NS	NS	NS	
Sovereign Centre	1011	1041	1111	1141	1241	1341	1411	1441	1511	1541	1611	1641
The Pier	1020	1050	1120	1150	1250	1350	1420	1450	1520	1550	1620	1650
Meads (St. Bedes School)	1027	1057	1127	1157	1257	1357	1427	1457	1527	1557	1627	1657
Top of Beachy Head	1035	1105	1135	1205	1305	1405	1435	1505	1535	1605	1635	1705

GO TO THE TOP OF BEACHY HEAD – 575 FEET ABOVE THE SEA!

							NS	NS	NS	NS	NS	
Top of Beachy Head	1040	1110	1140	1210	1310	1410	1440	1510	1540	1610	1640	1710
Meads (St. Bedes School)	1048	1118	1148	1218	1318	1418	1448	1518	1548	1618	1648	1718
The Pier	1055	1125	1155	1225	1325	1425	1455	1525	1555	1625	1655	1725
Sovereign Centre	1102	1132	1202	1232	1332	1432	1502	1532	1602	1632	1702	1732

★ – Starts from The Pier on Saturdays.   NS – Not on Saturdays.

Service 10 — CRUMBLES HARBOUR—SOVEREIGN CENTRE—TOWN CENTRE—FARLAINE ROAD

(Via Prince William Parade, Seafront, Pier, Upperton Road, The Goffs, High Street, Green Street, Victoria Drive)

Sundays & Bank Holidays only

Crumbles Harbour (Atlantic Way)		1023	1123	1223	1323	1423	1523	1623
Sovereign Centre		1025	1125	1225	1325	1425	1525	1625
The Pier		1032	1132	1232	1332	1432	1532	1632
Terminus Road ≠	arr.	1037	1137	1237	1337	1437	1537	1637
Terminus Road ≠	dep.	1040	1140	1240	1340	1440	1540	1640
Farlaine Road		1050	1150	1250	1350	1450	1550	1650

Farlaine Road		0955	1053	1153	1253	1353	1453	1553
Terminus Road ≠	arr.	1005	1103	1203	1303	1403	1503	1603
Terminus Road ≠	dep.	1005	1105	1205	1305	1405	1505	1605
The Pier		1010	1110	1210	1310	1410	1510	1610
Sovereign Centre		1017	1117	1217	1317	1417	1517	1617
Crumbles Harbour (Atlantic Way)		1020	1120	1220	1320	1420	1520	1620

≠ – Near to British Rail Station.   Service 1 also serves Farlaine Road and Service 3 operates along the Seafront.

ON 18th JULY, 1993, THE EASTBOURNE OMNIBUS SOCIETY WILL HOLD A BUS RALLY ON EASTBOURNE SEA FRONT

EASTBOURNE BUSES 1903–1993

As certificated by the "Guinness Book of Records" the world's first Municipal Motor Bus Service commenced operation in Eastbourne on 12th April, 1903.

From 12th June until 3rd October, 1993, there will be a special display at the Towner Art Gallery and Local History Museum, High Street, Old Town.

Map of principal bus routes and fare zones

Bus & Coach enquiries and ticket sales from our Bus Stop Shop situated in the Arndale Centre in the town centre

Eastbourne Buses Ltd, Transport Offices, Birch Road, Eastbourne BN23 6PD

Zone 1	Town Centre
Zone 2	Meads
Zone 3	Old Town
Zone 4	Hampden Park
Zone 5	Langney
Zone 6	Seaside

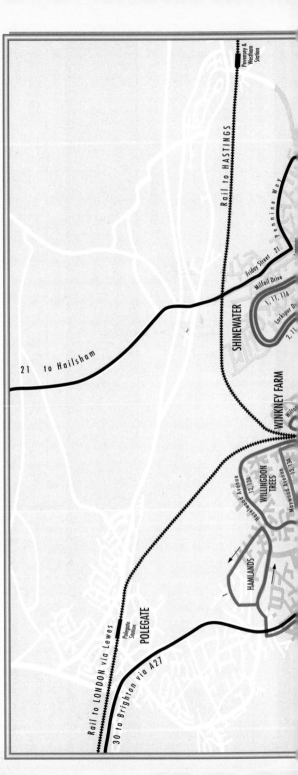

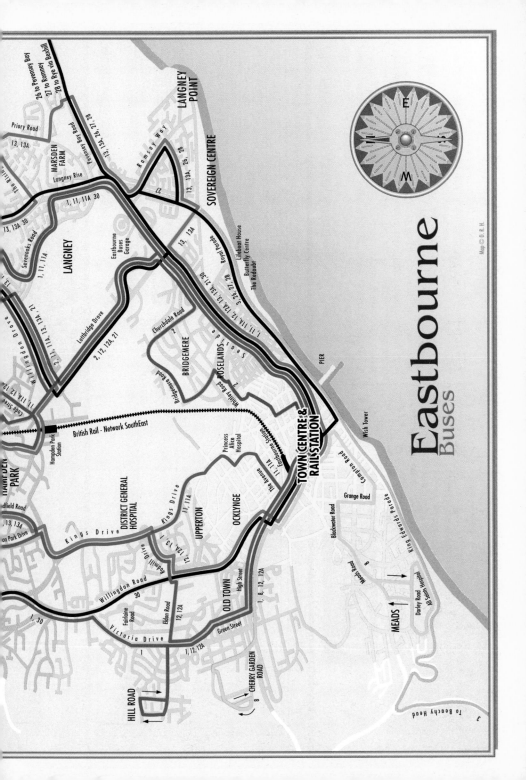

Eastbourne
Buses

Map © D.R.H.

N E W S (compass rose)

26 to Pevensey Bay
27 to Romney
28 to Rye via Bexhill

Priory Road

13, 13A

MARSDEN FARM

Langney Rise

The Kiln

Sevenoaks Road

13, 13A 30

1, 11, 11A

1, 11, 11A 30

LANGNEY

Eastbourne Buses Garage

Lottbridge Drove

2, 11, 11A, 13, 13A, 21

2, 11, 11A, 13, 13A, 21

Willingdon Drove

2, 12, 12A, 21

Churchdale Road

Bridgemere Road

BRIDGEMERE

2

ROSELANDS

Whitley Road

Seaside

Pevensey Bay Road

13, 13A, 26, 27, 28

13, 13A, 26, 27, 28

Ramsey Way

LANGNEY POINT

SOVEREIGN CENTRE

13, 13A

13, 13A

Royal Parade

Lifeboat House
Butterfly Centre
The Redoubt

1, 11, 11A, 12, 12A, 13, 13A, 21, 26, 28, 2, 3, 27, 28

Trade Street

11, 11A, 12, 12A

Hampden Park Station

British Rail - Network SouthEast

HAMPDEN PARK

dfield Road

13, 13A

on Park Drive

1, 30

Kings Drive

DISTRICT GENERAL HOSPITAL

Kings Drive

Redmill Drive

11, 11A

Willingdon Road

30

Fairlane Road

Victoria Drive

1

Eldon Road

12, 12A

UPPERTON

Princess Alice Hospital

The Avenue

11, 11A

11, 11A

OCKLYNGE

High Street

OLD TOWN

Green Street

1, 12, 12A

CHERRY GARDEN ROAD

8

HILL ROAD

Eastbourne Station

TOWN CENTRE & RAILSTATION

PIER

Wish Tower

Compton Road

Grange Road

Blackwater Road

Meads Road

1, 8, 12, 12A

8

Burlington Place

MEADS

Darley Road
All Saints Hospital

3 To Beachy Head

Service 8
CHERRY GARDEN ROAD—OLD TOWN—TOWN CENTRE—MEADS

(Via Manvers Road, Osborne Road, Longland Road, Church Street, The Goffs, Upperton Road, Devonshire Place, Compton Street, Silverdale Road, Grange Road, Blackwater Road, Meads Road, Meads Street, Darley Road, Dukes Drive). Some journeys are operated by Southdown Motor Services.

Mondays to Saturdays only

					Then at these minutes past each hour			
Cherry Garden Road		—	0804	0834	04	34	1804	—
Terminus Road ⇌	arr.	—	0815	0845	15	45	1815	—
Terminus Road ⇌	dep.	0748	0818	0848	18	48	1818	1918
Winter Garden		0752	0822	0852	22	52	1822	1922
Meads (St. Bedes School)		0802	0832	0902	32	02	1832	1932

(Column markers between "minutes past each hour" and the evening times read **UNTIL**.)

		MF	MF	S				Then at these minutes past each hour			
Meads (St. Bedes School)		0711	0736	—	0806	0836	0906	36	06	1806	1936
Winter Garden		0720	0745	—	0815	0845	0915	45	15	1815	1945
Terminus Road ⇌	arr.	0724	0748	—	0819	0849	0919	49	19	1819	1949
Terminus Road ⇌	dep.	0724	0748		0752	0822	0852	0922	52	22	—	—
Cherry Garden Road		—			0803	0833	0903	0933	03	33	—	—

S – Operates on Saturdays only. ⇌ – Near to British Rail Station. MF – Additional journey on Mondays to Fridays.

NO SUNDAY SERVICE.

BUS FARES IN EASTBOURNE

Eastbourne is divided into six 'Fare Zones'. Fares are based on travel within one zone or travel within two or more adjacent zones. A separate leaflet is available free of charge describing fares and zones in detail. You may purchase from the bus driver Single or Twelvecard tickets for which payment must be in cash. Twelvecard tickets can also be obtained at the Town Centre Bus Stop Shop for cash or by credit card. Senior Citizens may obtain reduced Single tickets during eligible times if in possession of a Countycard. Children between 5 and 13 years of age (5 and 15 years on schooldays) travel at child rate until 1900 hours every day. Accompanied Children under 5 years of age travel free. Dogs are charged a flat fare.

EAST SUSSEX COUNTYCARD

Countycard entitles you to reduced off peak bus travel for all bus journeys that start or finish in East Sussex. It is available to Senior Citizens, Students (aged 16-18) and the physically or mentally handicapped. It is valid after 0900 hours Mondays to Fridays and all day at Weekends or Bank Holidays. There is a charge made for issue available free to Blind Persons. You may obtain a leaflet and application form from Bus Company offices or your local Council. The scheme is administered for East Sussex County Council.

Service 1 — SHINEWATER—LANGNEY—TOWN CENTRE—OLD TOWN—HILL ROAD/FARLAINE ROAD—HAMLANDS

(Via Larkspur Drive, Milfoil Drive, Sevenoaks Road, Langney Rise, St. Anthonys Avenue, Seaside, Memorial Roundabout, Upperton Road, The Goffs, High Street, Church Street, Green Street, Victoria Drive, Willingdon Road, Huggetts Lane, Seven Sisters Road)

Mondays to Saturdays

Outward journeys (Shinewater → Hamlands)

Stop										Then at these minutes past each hour									Sundays
	X	MF																	
Birch Road (Bus Garage)	0552	0619	–	–	–					32	A	02	A			–	–	1924	0946
Shinewater (Milfoil Drive)	0559	0626	0659	–	–	0729	0739	0759	0809	0829	39 57 A 09 27 A	1729 1759 1829 1849 1931							0951
Langney (Shopping Centre)	0603	0630	0703	0713	0733	0743	0803	0813	0833	43 03 13 33	1733 1803 1833 1853 1935								0955
Langney Rise (Martello)	0607	0634	0707	0717	0737	0747	0807	0817	0837	47 07 17 37	1737 1807 1837 1857 1939								0959
Seaside (Alexandra Arms)	0611	0643	0711	0721	0741	0751	0811	0821	0841	51 11 21 41	1741 1811 1841 1901 1943								1003
Terminus Road ≆ arr.	0623	0655	0723	0733	0753	0803	0823	0833	0853	03 23 33 53	1753 1823 1853 1913 1955								1012
Terminus Road ≆ dep.	0627	0657	0727	0737	0757	0807	0827	0837	0857	07 27 37 57	1757 1827 1855 –								1955
Hill Road	0638	–	0708	–	–	–	–	–	–	– 38 – 08	1808 1838 1905 –								–
Farlaine Road ★	–	0708	–	0748	0808	0818	–	–	–	18 48 – 08	1808 1838 1905 2005								–
Willingdon Roundabout	0620	0650	0720	–	0751	0807	0821	0837	0851	21 51	1811 – – –								–
Hamlands (Shops)	–	–	–	0758	–	0828	–	–	0858	28 58	1818 – – –								–

Return journeys (Hamlands → Shinewater/Birch Road)

Stop										Then at these minutes past each hour									Sundays
		MF																	
Hamlands (Shops)	–	–	0800	–	–	–	–	0830	–	00 30	–	–	1730	1800 1820		–			–
Willingdon Roundabout	–	–	0807	–	0821	–	–	0837	–	07 37	–	–	1737	1807 1827 1846		–			–
Farlaine Road ★	0620	0650	0720	0750	0810	0820	0840	–	0850	10 20 40	50	–	1740	1810 1830 1849		–			1653
Hill Road	–	–	0750	–	–	–	–	–	–	–	–	–	1750	–		–			–
Terminus Road ≆ dep.	0632	0702	0732	0802	0822	0832	0852	0902	–	22 32 52 02	1752	1802	1822	1842 1859		1703			–
Seaside (Arlington Arms)	0635	0705	0735	0745	0802	0833	0833	0853	0903	23 33 53 03	1753	1802	1825	1842 1901		1705			–
Langney Rise (opp. Martello)	0644	0714	0744	0754	0814	0834	0844	0904	0914	34 44 04 14	1804	1814	1834	1851 1910		1714			–
Langney (Shopping Centre)	0648	0718	0748	0758	0818	0838	0848	0908	0918	38 48 18	1808	1818	1838	BR 1914		1718			–
Shinewater (Shopping Centre)	0653	0723	0753	0803	0823	0843	0853	0913	0923	43 53 13 23	1813	1823	1843	– 1919		1723			–
Shinewater (Milfoil Drive)	0657	0727	0757	0807	0827	0847	0857	0917	A	47 59 17 29	1817	1827	1847	– –		1727			–
Birch Road (Bus Garage)	–	–	–	–	0854	–	–	–	0924	54 A 24 A	1824	–	–	– –		1734			–

≆ Near to British Rail Station. ★ Journeys start/terminate at Ocklynge School, journeys to/from Hamlands pass end of road. Services 2 & 10 also serve Farlaine Road.

For additional buses between Langney Rise (Martello) and Terminus Road see Services 11/11A. For additional buses from Shinewater see Services 2 & 11/11A.

For additional buses between Terminus Road and Old Town see Services 12/12A. X – Operates via Ramsay Way & Sovereign Centre. BR – To Birch Road Bus Garage.

A – Journeys to and from Shinewater mostly as Service 2. MF – Operates Mondays to Fridays.

Services 26 / 28

BEACHLANDS—PEVENSEY BAY—EASTBOURNE
(Via Coast Road, Pevensey Bay Road, Langney Point, Seafront)

RYE—BATTLE—BEXHILL—PEVENSEY BAY—EASTBOURNE
(Via A268, Cripps Corner, London Road, A259, Pevensey Bay Road, Langney Point, Seafront)
Including Sunday journeys on Service 27

The following table groups the columns into **Mondays to Fridays**, **Saturdays** and **Sundays** (Service 27). Each column is headed by its service number.

Stop	MtoF 28	MtoF 26	MtoF 28	MtoF 26	MtoF 28	MtoF 26	MtoF 28	MtoF 26	MtoF 28	MtoF 28	MtoF 28	Sat 28	Sat 28	Sat 28	Sat 28	Sat 28	Sat 28	Sun 27	Sun 27
Rye (Rail Station) ⇥	–	–	–	–	–	–	1213	–	1433	–	1813	0813	–	1213	–	1543	1813	1332	1632
Peasmarsh (Post Office)	–	–	–	–	–	–	1223	–	1443	–	1823	0823	–	1223	–	1553	1823	–	–
Beckley (Rose & Crown)	–	–	–	–	★	–	1232	–	1452	–	1832	0832	–	1232	–	1602	1832	–	–
Northiam (K & ESR Station)	–	–	–	–	1039	–	1239	–	1459	–	1839	0839	1039	1239	–	1609	1839	–	–
Sandhurst (The Green)	–	–	–	–	1044	–	1244	–	1504	–	1844	0844	1044	1244	–	1614	1844	–	–
Bodiam Castle	–	–	–	–	1049	–	1249	–	1509	–	1849	0849	1049	1249	–	1619	1849	–	–
Staplecross (The Stores)	–	–	–	–	1054	–	1254	–	1514	–	1854	0854	1054	1254	–	1624	1854	–	–
Sedlescombe (The Green)	–	–	–	–	1059	–	1259	–	1519	–	1859	0859	1059	1259	–	1629	1859	–	–
Battle (Abbey)	–	–	0909	–	1109	–	1309	–	1529	1739	1909	0909	1109	1309	1509	1639	1909	–	–
Catsfield (White Hart)	–	–	0919	–	1119	–	1319	–	1539	1749	1919	0919	1119	1319	1519	1649	1919	–	–
Ninfield (The Kings Arms)	–	–	0922	–	1122	–	1322	–	1542	1752	1922	0922	1122	1322	1522	1652	1922	–	–
Sidley (Sussex Hotel)	–	–	0931	–	1131	–	1331	–	1551	1801	1931	0931	1131	1331	1531	1701	1931	–	–
Bexhill (Town Hall Square) ⇥	–	–	0938	–	1138	–	1338	–	1558	1808	1938	0938	1138	1338	1538	1708	1938	1429	1729
Little Common (Roundabout)	–	–	0945	–	1145	–	1345	–	1605	1815	1945	0945	1145	1345	1545	1715	1945	1435	1735
Pevensey (Bridge End) ⇥	0758	–	0958	–	1158	–	1358	–	1618	1828	1958	0958	1158	1358	1558	1728	1958	1445	1745
Beachlands (Marine Avenue)	–	0856	–	1056	–	1256	–	1456	–	–	–	–	–	–	–	–	–	–	–
Pevensey Bay (St. Wilfrids Church)	0800	0900	1000	1100	1200	1300	1400	1500	1620	1830	2000	1000	1200	1400	1600	1730	2000	1447	1747
Crumbles Centre (Asda)	0804	0904	1004	1104	1204	1304	1404	1504	1624	1834	2004	1004	1204	1404	1604	1734	2004	1451	1751
Ramsay Way	0806	0906	1006	1106	1206	1306	1406	1506	1626	1836	2006	1006	1206	1406	1606	1736	2006	–	–
Sovereign Centre	0809	0909	1009	1109	1209	1309	1409	1509	1629	1839	2009	1009	1209	1409	1609	1739	2009	1454	1754
The Pier	0816	0916	1016	1116	1216	1316	1416	1516	1636	1846	2016	1016	1216	1416	1616	1746	2016	1500	1800
Eastbourne (Terminus Road) ⇥	0821	0921	1021	1121	1221	1321	1421	1521	1641	1851	2021	1021	1221	1421	1621	1751	2021	1505	1805

Sundays (Service 27): "From New Romney via Hastings" — the Rye journeys (1332, 1632) reach Bexhill via Hastings; intermediate stops between Rye and Bexhill are not served.

⇥ – Near to British Rail Station.   ★ – Starts from Goddens Gill 3 minutes earlier.

Service 30 EASTBOURNE—POLEGATE—BRIGHTON

(Via Langney Rise, Seaside, A22, A27, Lewes Road, North Street)

Mondays to Fridays and Sundays – journeys operated by Eastbourne Buses. Saturdays – journeys operated by Brighton Buses.

Mondays to Fridays

					Saturdays			Sundays	
Eastbourne (Langney Shopping Centre) ⇌	0715	–	1245	1615	1030	–	1725	1045	1545
Eastbourne (Terminus Road) ⇌	0735	1005	1305	1635	1050	1250	1745	1105	1605
Polegate (Harvesters Cross Roads) ⇌	0746	1016	1316	1646	1101	1301	1756	1116	1616
Berwick Roundabout (for Drusillas Zoo)	0751	1021	1321	1651	1106	1306	1801	1121	1621
University of Sussex, A27 LIMITED	0810	1040	1340	1710	1125	1325	1820	1140	1640
Brighton (Old Steine – Stop G) STOP	0824	1054	1354	1724	1139	1339	1834	1154	1654
Brighton (Churchill Square) SECTION	0827	1057	1357	1727	1142	1342	1837	1157	1657

					Saturdays			Sundays	
Brighton (Churchill Square – Stop E)	0910	1110	1410	1740	0910	1150	1610	1210	1710
Brighton (Old Steine – Stop F) LIMITED	0913	1113	1413	1743	0913	1153	1613	1213	1713
University of Sussex, A27 STOP SECTION	0927	1127	1427	1757	0927	1207	1627	1227	1727
Berwick Roundabout (for Drusillas Zoo) ⇌	0942	1142	1442	1812	0942	1222	1642	1242	1742
Polegate (Harvesters Cross Roads) ⇌	0947	1147	1447	1817	0947	1227	1647	1247	1747
Eastbourne (Terminus Road) ⇌	1002	1202	1502	1832	1002	1242	1702	1302	1802
Eastbourne (Langney Shopping Centre)	–	1222	1522	1852	1022	–	1722	1322	1822

ON BANK & PUBLIC HOLIDAYS

Generally a Sunday Service timetable will be operated. Please check before travelling on these days.

LOST PROPERTY

Please check you have not left anything behind. If you think you have left anything behind phone us on Eastbourne 416416 Mondays to Fridays 0900-1615 hours. Property can be collected from our Birch Road offices during these hours.

Use SERVICE 30 to visit DRUSILLAS ZOO

A short walk from Berwick Roundabout

⇌ – Near to British Rail Station.   Fare savings for regular travellers with a 12 journey discount ticket, between Eastbourne or Polegate and Brighton.

LIMITED STOP SECTION: Between Sussex University and Churchill Square this service stops only at Stanmer Park Gates, Coldean Lane, The Avenue, Bear Road, Elm Grove and St Peters Church, in addition to the timetable stops.

NO ADVANCE BOOKING ON THIS SERVICE. Return tickets issued by Eastbourne Buses will be accepted by Brighton Buses and vice-versa.

Brighton   Home of Britain's oldest electric railway   **1883-1993**

VOLKS ELECTRIC RAILWAY – Aquarium to Marina

Services 11/11A HAMPDEN PARK—SHINEWATER—LANGNEY—TOWN CENTRE—GENERAL HOSPITAL—HAMPDEN PARK

(Via Lottbridge Drove, Willingdon Drove, Larkspur Drive, Milfoil Drive, Sevenoaks Road, St. Anthonys Avenue, Seaside, The Avenue, Enys Road, Lewes Road, Kings Drive, Decoy Drive, Lindfield Road, Brodrick Road, Brassey Avenue, Mountfield Road)

11 – CLOCKWISE CIRCULAR SERVICE   11A – ANTI-CLOCKWISE CIRCULAR SERVICE

Mondays to Saturdays

Service No. 11

Brodrick Road (Henfield Road)	–	–	0736	0806		36	06	1706	1736	1804	–	1955	2055	2155	
Hampden Park Station ⇌	–	–	0739	0809		39	09	1709	1739	1807	–	1958	2058	2158	
The Hydneye (Cade Street)	–	–	0741	0811		41	11	1711	1741	–	1900	2000	2100	2200	
Shinewater (Milfoil Drive)	–	–	0749	0819	Then at	49	19	1719	1749	–	1905	2005	2105	2205	Then at
Langney (Shopping Centre)	0657	0727	0753	0823	these	53	23	1723	1753	–	1910	2010	2110	2210	these
Langney Rise (Martello)	0701	0731	0757	0827	minutes	57	27	1727	1757	–	1914	2014	2114	2214	minutes
Seaside (Alexandra Arms)	0706	0736	0801	0831	past	01	31	1731	1801	–	1918	2018	2118	2218	past
Terminus Road ⇌ arr.	0718	0748	0813	0843	each	13	43	1743	1813	–	1928	2028	2128	2228	each
Terminus Road ⇌ dep.	0720	0750	0818	0848	hour	18	48	1748	–	–	1938	2038	2138	2238	hour
Kings Drive (General Hospital)	0729	0759	0827	0857		27	57	1757	–	–	1946	2046	2146	2246	
Brodrick Road (Henfield Road)	0736	0806	0834	0904		34	04	1804	–	–	1952	2052	2152	2252	
												★			

Service No. 11A

	MF★	MF		★	MF											
Brodrick Road (Henfield Road)	0700	–	0752	0826	0831	0852	Then at	22	52	1722	1752	1822	1939	2040	2140	2240
Kings Drive (General Hospital)	0706	–	0800	0833	0839	0900	these	30	00	1730	1800	1830	1946	2046	2146	2246
Terminus Road ⇌ arr.	0715	–	0809	0842	0848	0909	minutes	39	09	1739	1809	1839	1954	2054	2154	2254
Terminus Road ⇌ dep.	0715	–	0813	0843	–	0913	past	43	13	1743	1810	1843	2003	2103	2203	2303
Seaside (Arlington Arms)	0724	0805	0824	0854	–	0924	each	54	24	1754	1819	1856	2012	2112	2212	2312
Langney Rise (Martello)	0728	0809	0828	0858	–	0928	hour	58	28	1758	1823	1856	2016	2116	2216	2316
Langney (Shopping Centre)	0733	0814	0833	0903	–	0933		03	33	1803	1828	1901	2021	2121	2221	2321
Shinewater (Milfoil Drive)	0737	0818	0837	0907	–	0937		07	37	1807	–	1905	2025	2125	2225	2325
The Hydneye (Cade Street)	0745	0826	0845	0915	–	0945		15	45	1815	–	–	2034	2134	2234	2334
Hampden Park Station ⇌	0747	0828	0847	0917	–	0947		17	47	1817	–	–	2036	2136	2236	–
Brodrick Road (Henfield Road)	0750	0831	0850	0920	–	0950		20	50	1820	–	–	2037	2137	2237	–

MF – Additional journey on Mondays to Fridays.   ⇌ Near to British Rail Station.   ★ – To or from Hampden Park Station (Lottbridge Arms).

For additional buses serving The Hydneye and Hampden Park Station see Services 12/12A.   For additional buses serving Shinewater and Langney Rise see Service 1.

Sundays

Service No. 11

Brodrick Road (Henfield Road)	–	1055	55	2155	
Hampden Park Station ⇌	–	1058	58	2158	
The Hydneye (Cade Street)	–	1100	00	2200	
Shinewater (Milfoil Drive)	1005	1105	05	2205	Then at
Langney (Shopping Centre)	1010	1110	10	2210	these
Langney Rise (Martello)	1014	1114	14	2214	minutes
Seaside (Alexandra Arms)	1018	1118	18	2218	past
Terminus Road ⇌	1028	1128	28	2228	each
Terminus Road ⇌	1038	1138	38	2238	hour
Kings Drive (General Hospital)	1046	1146	46	2246	
Brodrick Road (Henfield Road)	1052	1152	52	2252	
				★	

Service No. 11A

Brodrick Road (Henfield Road)	–	1040	40	2240	
Kings Drive (General Hospital)	–	1046	46	2246	
Terminus Road ⇌	–	1054	54	2254	
Terminus Road ⇌	–	1103	03	2303	Then at
Seaside (Arlington Arms)	–	1112	12	2312	these
Langney Rise (Martello)	–	1116	16	2316	minutes
Langney (Shopping Centre)	1021	1121	21	2321	past
Shinewater (Milfoil Drive)	1025	1125	25	2325	each
The Hydneye (Cade Street)	1034	1134	34	2334	hour
Hampden Park Station ⇌	1036	1136	36	–	
Brodrick Road (Henfield Road)	1037	1137	37	–	

★ – To or from Hampden Park Station (Lottbridge Arms).

For additional buses serving Shinewater and Langney Rise see Service 1.

Services 21 — EASTBOURNE—LANGNEY—STONE CROSS—HAILSHAM
(Via Seaside, Birch Road, Willingdon Drove, Hide Hollow, Pennine Way, B2104)

268 — EASTBOURNE—LANGNEY—STONE CROSS—HAILSHAM—HORAM—HEATHFIELD SCHOOL
(Via Seaside, Birch Road, Willingdon Drove, Hide Hollow, Pennine Way, B2104, Grove Bridge, B2203)

Mondays to Fridays / Saturdays

	Mondays to Fridays					Saturdays		
Service No.	21	268 (LR)	21	21	21	21	21	21
Eastbourne (Terminus Road) ✠	–	–	1005	1330	1645	1025	1355	1545
Seaside (Arlington Arms)	–	–	1014	1339	1654	1034	1404	1554
Birch Road (Bus Garage)	0707	–	1016	1341	1656	1036	1406	1556
Langney (Shopping Centre)	0713	–	1022	1347	1702	1042	1412	1602
Pennine Way	0716	–	1025	1350	1705	1045	1415	1605
Stone Cross (Red Lion)	0719	–	1028	1353	1708	1048	1418	1608
Hailsham (North Street)	0729	0845	1038	1403	1718	1058	1428	1618
Hellingly Hospital Entrance	–	0855	–	–	–	–	–	–
Horam (Merrydown Winery)	–	0903	–	–	–	–	–	–
Heathfield School	–	0913	–	–	–	–	–	–

Mondays to Fridays / Saturdays

	Mondays to Fridays					Saturdays		
Service No.	21	21	21	268 (LR)	21	21	21	21
Heathfield School	–	–	–	1600	–	–	–	–
Horam (Merrydown Winery)	–	–	–	1610	–	–	–	–
Hellingly Hospital Entrance	–	–	–	1618	–	–	–	–
Hailsham (High Street)	0735	0843	1043	1625	1723	1105	–	1625
Stone Cross (opp. Red Lion)	0745	0853	1053	1635	1733	1115	–	1635
Pennine Way	0748	0856	1056	1638	1736	1118	1327	1638
Langney (Shopping Centre)	0751	0859	1059	1641	1739	1121	1330	1641
Birch Road (Bus Garage)	0757	0905	1105	1647	1745	1127	1336	1647
Seaside (Alexandra Arms)	0759	0907	1107	1649	1747	1129	1338	1649
Eastbourne (Terminus Road) ✠	0811	0919	1119	1701	1759	1141	1350	1701

✠ – Near to British Rail Station.   LR – Local Rider journeys between Heathfield School and Hailsham.   **NO SUNDAY SERVICE.**

SUPPORT EASTBOURNE'S LIFEBOAT

Eastbourne Buses Ltd is pleased to support our Local Lifeboat and Crew

INDEX

We use the 24-hour clock for all bus timetables in this leaflet. This is to avoid confusion between am and pm services. 1 am becomes 0100 hours, 2 am becomes 0200 hours and so on until after midday (1200) when 1 pm becomes 1300 hours etc.

Destination	Service No.
All Saints Hospital	3, 8
Appledore Station ⇌	27
Battle ⇌	28
Beachlands	26
Beachy Head	3
Beckley	28
Bexhill ⇌	27, 28
Birch Road	2, 12, 12A, 21, 268
Bodiam Castle	28
Bridgemere	2
Brighton	30
Catsfield	28
Cherry Garden Road	8
Crumbles Centre	13, 13A, 26, 27, 28
Crumbles Harbour	10
Drusillas Zoo	30
Eastbourne Buses Garage	1, 2, 12, 12A, 21, 268
Eastbourne Rail Station ⇌	1, 2, 8, 10, 11, 11A, 12, 12A, 13, 13A, 21, 26, 27, 28, 30

Destination	Service No.
Farlaine Road	1, 2, 10
General Hospital	11, 11A, 12, 12A, 13, 13A
Guestling	27
Hailsham	21, 268
Hamlands	1
Hampden Park Station ⇌	11, 11A, 12, 12A, 13, 13A
Hastings	27
Heathfield School	268
Hellingly	268
Hill Road	1
Horam	268
Hydneye	11, 11A, 12, 12A
Kent & East Sussex Railway	28
Langney Martello	1, 11, 11A, 30
Langney Shopping Centre	1, 2, 11, 11A, 13, 13A, 21, 30, 268
Little Common	27, 28
Lunsford Cross	28
Maywood Avenue	13, 13A
Meads	3, 8

Destination	Service No.
New Romney	27
Ninfield	28
Northiam	28
Ore	27
Peasmarsh	28
Pennine Way ⇌	21, 268
Pevensey	27, 28
Pevensey Bay	26, 27, 28
Pier (Eastbourne)	3, 10, 26, 27, 28
Polegate	30
Princess Alice Hospital	11, 11A
Ramsay Way	13, 13A, 26, 28
Rising	13, 13A
Romney Railway	27
Rye ⇌	27, 28
Seafront	3, 10, 26, 27, 28
Seaside	1, 11, 11A, 12, 12A, 13, 13A, 21, 30, 268
Sedlescombe	28
Shinewater	1, 2, 11, 11A
Sovereign Centre	3, 10, 13, 13A, 26, 27, 28
Stone Cross	21, 268
St. Leonards	27
University of Sussex	30
Willingdon Roundabout	1, 30
Willingdon Trees	12, 12A
Winchelsea	27
Winkney Farm Estate	12, 12A
Winter Garden	8

⇌ Eastbourne Buses provide connecting facilities with British Rail (Network South-East) trains at Appledore, Battle, Bexhill, Eastbourne, Hampden Park, Pevensey Bay, Rye and St. Leonards Stations.

For rail enquiries Telephone 0273-206755 or 0424-429325.

Produced by Prime Print, England. Tel: Eastbourne (0323) 482819

65. Southdown's Eastbourne operations were just part of a fleet of around 900 vehicles spread from Hampshire to Kent. Here is No 727 (LUF227) working the 126 to Seaford.

a bonus for Southdown. The availability of the somewhat spartan utility vehicles made them likely candidates for conversion to open toppers, 412 being decapitated in April 51. The 5LW was not up to the climb to Beachy Head, so a more powerful 6LW engine was quickly fitted. In this condition it passes the end of Terminus Road on the 92 proceeding along the seafront to the layby at Beach Head constructed in 1950.

Route 97 was reintroduced after the war in time for Christmas 1945 and by the mid fifties it was an all year hourly service rising to a seasonal peak of 15 minutes in fine weather. In the summer season route 197 offered a twice hourly return trip of 50 minutes via Birling Gap and East Dean, frequency being reduced off season when it was curtailed to run to Birling Gap and back.

Picture 62 shows Langney Road in the early fifties and Southdown No 113 as a relief on route 12 indicating the level of use made of this important route across the Downs. It ran three times an hour via Seaford and Newhaven. The inland alternative via Lewes was hourly. The vehicle was new in 1935 as a Leyland TD4c with a Short 50 seat body. It had its petrol engine replaced with an 8.6 Leyland oil engine and its torque converter removed around the time of its rebodying. The new East Lancs body gave two extra seats and a modern appearance and it was amongst the last of the 1935 vintage vehicles to be withdrawn in 1961. Fares from Eastbourne to Brighton would be 2/6p (12p) single or 4/- (20p) return.

Parked outside Royal Parade garage in Picture 63 is No 271 (GUF671) which displays its distinctly utility origins, being new in July 1946 with Park Royal Highbridge bodywork. It displays a screen for service 95 which ran from the Star Inn, Waldron via Heathfield and Hailsham with six journeys daily each taking 1 hr 24 mins. By the end of the decade most trips ran only between Hailsham and Waldron. No 271 was withdrawn in 1963. The livery retains lining out in dark green which sits neatly on the angular body. Billboard, bus and depot carry similar styles of "Southdown", an instantly recognised feature before the concept of corporate images.

Seen in the mid 1950s in Picture 64 is Southdown No 1131 (CCD731) taking the short but scenic route to Wannock, where visitors could enjoy a leisurely afternoon at the Tea Gardens. Southdown was by then famous for its extensive programme of tours and excursions having taken over the licences of several Eastbourne operators before the war, the first being Harvey in September 1939. This particular vehicle is a Leyland TS7 Tiger with 32 seat Beadle coach body delivered new in 1939. Many Southdown coaches had their lives extended by rebuilding but other than an oil engine fitted in 1950 but 1131 is as purchased. During the war years it had served as an ambulance with seating removed.

Reliefs were commonplace in the fifties. In Picture 65 No 727 (LUF227) is working the 126 to Seaford. The cycles propped against Diplocks Hotel indicate the low level of car ownership in the early post war years. Large batches of Leylands were arriving enabling utility vehicles to be replaced. No 727 is a PD2/12 with a Leyland

66. Southdown No 164 with Park Royal bodywork from the late 1940s passes the site where Barclays Bank is being rebuilt after wartime destruction.

67. The livery on this Maidstone & District AEC Regent V was similar to the pre World War II standard although gold lining was no longer carried. Maidstone & District vehicles in their darker green contrasted quite dramatically with Southdown's brighter colour.

body seating 58, it has a triple route number box and arrived in December 1951 fitted with an enclosed platform but without doors which were installed the next year. The high standards maintained by the company are evident from the uniforms. Operations in Eastbourne must be considered within the context of an operator which provided services from Hampshire to Kent, with a fleet approaching 900 vehicles. The Eastbourne operating area contained eight depots and dormy sheds, consisting of Pevensey Road, Royal Parade, Alfriston, Crowborough, Dicker, Heathfield, Seaford and Uckfield.

In Picture 66 is No 164 (EUF164), a Leyland TD5 fitted with a Park Royal Lowbridge body new in 1938. The body was removed in April 1949 and the 54 seater Park Royal body shown took its place. Barclays Bank is undergoing reconstruction and parking on Terminus Road is restricted to one side only, alternating daily. The vestiges of the original villas can be seen above the shop frontages added later. Service 25 left Eastbourne regularly at 10 minutes to the hour and travelled to Brighton via Polegate, Berwick and Lewes taking 1 hr 33 mins.

Maidstone and District fleet received 22 AEC Regent Vs in 1956 of which 14 had full height bodies by Park Royal. The bodywork on DH479 (VKR471) in Picture 67 looks well balanced with the additional cream bands and green lining, although this had been abandoned in the war years it was reintroduced and buses continued to be finished in this style until 1957. Other than the loss of gold lining and the painting of roofs in dark colours in the war, the Maidstone & District double deckers looked little different from vehicles thirty years earlier. Route 15 still ran jointly with Southdown. During the war an extra nine minutes had been allowed for running in the blackout but an hourly service was maintained with just the suspension of Sunday morning journeys for two years. By the time this view was taken the route was running every half hour in the summer season, being reduced to hourly in the winter.

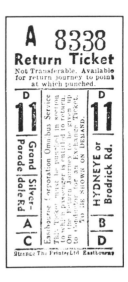

5. THE SIXTIES - YEARS OF CONSOLIDATION

No 19 (JK9117) was unique in the Eastbourne fleet being the sole AEC Regent II. Delivered in 1946, it was to serve for nearly twenty one years outlasting many of the later Regent IIIs of 1947. By the time Picture 68 was taken, all routes had been numbered, the interworking of the Old Town (1) and Ocklynge (4) routes dated back to the thirties when construction of Eldon Road made circular working of the two routes possible. At the other end of the town the development of Langney at first utilised the Friday Street buses passing along Langney Rise but by the end of the fifties the Priory Road and Marsden Road terminus had been established.

In Picture 69 the conductor of No 20 (JK9048) pauses for a chat with his driver whilst waiting at Cherry Garden Road on the edge of the South Downs, before heading back down to the railway station. The Weymann bodied AEC Regent III of 1947 is similar to vehicles running in Brighton at this time. With its fluted skirts the Weymann body looks dated compared with East Lancs models delivered the next year. All the 1948 batch were withdrawn along with No 20 in April 1966.

Development on the Downs remains a controversial subject but bus services followed potential custom and by 1938 had extended to Cherry Garden Road. The history of this route had its origins with extensions of the Old Town service to Summerdown Road which housed convalescent soldiers in the First World War. By the start of the thirties a service connected Langney with East Dean Road although services to this part of Old Town were later commenced at Devonshire Park. By 1947 service No 1 as it was numbered started at Langney or Grand Parade.

In Picture 70 No 27 (JK9984) one of three Leyland PD2/1s delivered in 1948 is seen on route 10 in the early sixties. With East Lancs bodywork it lasted for nearly twenty years before withdrawal in 1968. Never the most photographed service, routes to Carew Road and Mill Road had their origins in services which proceeded along the Avenue in 1906 although prior to the great war the area was served only by passing services to Hampden Park. By 1914 Carew Road had become the destination of a route commencing from the Lodge and by the thirties had extended to Langney. This foreshadowed service 4a which when introduced in 1968 traversed the Tanbridge (Langney) to Ocklynge route. Meanwhile for nearly two decades the service which was to be numbered 10 provided an hourly service between the station and Mill Road (circa 1950-68).

No 48 (AHC448) in Picture 71 is the epitome of post war traditional bus design, being an AEC Regent III with body completed by East Lancs subsidiary Bruce. It is standing at the back of the Devonshire Swimming Baths which used seawater filled by tidal movements via a pipe under the seafront. Corporation bus services once provided comprehensive services for the nearby theatres, although a premium was charged for late evening buses. In earlier times special tickets were issued for such workings. No 48 is laying over whilst working service 9 which ran from Devonshire Park to Hampden Park. The 1960s saw consistently high standards of service; in

68. Unique in the Corporation bus fleet was No 19, an AEC Regent II dating from 1946. It is seen in Priory Road working to the Marsden Road terminus.

69. Cherry Garden Road is on the edge of the South Downs and provides the location for No 20 (JK9048), a Weymann bodied AEC Regent III of 1947.

70. Leyland PD2 No 27 is working route 10 which ran hourly between the station and Mill Road.

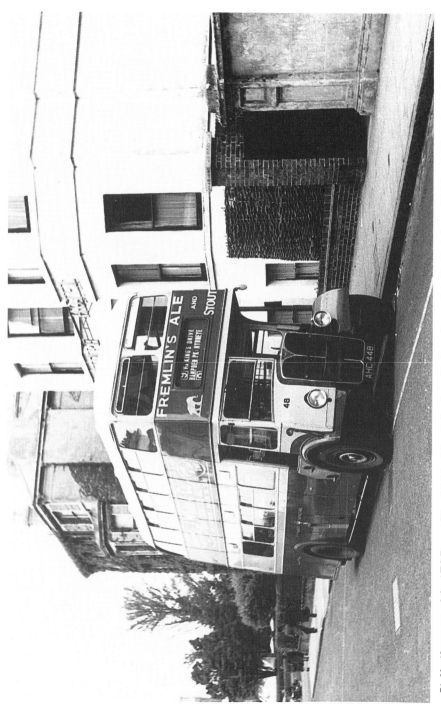

71. No **48** was one of the AEC Regent IIIs which had the distinction of bodywork completed in East Lancs Welsh subsidiary, Bruce Coachworks.

this case two buses an hour left for both Brodrick Road and The Hydneye. Other services served Hampden Park and also left from Devonshire Park. They were the 7 and 7A, both hourly to Brodrick Road which went via Ocklynge and Old Town respectively, thence by Willingdon Road etc. In 1965 the opening of Lottbridge Drove to traffic saw the commencement of services 14 and 14A which offered an alternative route from Hampden Park to Ocklynge and the station.

Picture 72 is dominated by St Marys parish church. No 54 (DHC654) is followed by Southdown 1605 (LUF605) whilst Eastbourne No 30 (JK9987) heads for Downs Avenue. A picture which is permeated with history set against the backdrop of the Downs. When Eastbourne was created the assembly rooms above the Lamb Inn served as the "Town Hall". Old Town retains some of its sites of antiquity, The Lamb being one of the oldest public houses in Britain. To the left of the picture stands the Towner Art Gallery and Museum amidst the Manor Gardens and Gildredge Park. At the heart of the area surrounded by cottages stood the Star Brewery which became redundant shortly after this photograph was taken. Its subsequent demolition after years of dereliction along with many of the towns oldest roads and houses remains a source of bitter memories. Through its narrow streets the stage coach had rattled and horses struggled their short lives hauling omnibuses up its steep hills.

No 54 which was to have a relatively short career was one of a batch of seven AEC Regent V 2D3RVs delivered in 1956, its 60 seat body was again from East Lancs coachbuilders. Looking at No 54 it is noticeably wider than No 30 at 8ft compared with the 7ft 6in of the latter. These vehicles with their "tin fronts" represented the final era of open platform buses in British bus design, although the famous AEC triangle still graced the grill. Detail changes to note are the route numbers which are now set in white blocks as opposed to the outline square on No 30.

Finally we can see the used ticket box which was eagerly emptied by young "bus spotters". Tickets had a relatively short history, until the late eighteenth century conductors often handed over the expected days takings, any surplus was pocketed. The introduction of tickets as well as controlling revenue and recording fares provided a useful source of advertising revenue. Early tickets were printed with the various stages of a particular route, the conductor punched them at the point of boarding, many designs following most printed locally. Machines which were in use in the 1960s were replaced by sophisticated equipment brought about by one person operation but the old ones found a new lease of life with seafront deck chair attendants.

Withdrawn in 1970, No 54 failed to outlive many of the Regent IIIs of earlier vintage. Nearing retirement was Southdown 1605 which had been new in 1952 and carried a rather ugly Duple coach body seating 41. It was withdrawn in 1964.

Routes to and from Old Town in the 1960s included journeys every 10 minutes from Langney via both Old Town and Ocklyne thence by Eldon Road giving the 1/4 seen on destinations. Service 2 also ran every 10 minutes from St Philips Avenue to Downs Avenue extended later to Newick Road, in 1967 the 2a commenced running an hourly service to the Green Street Farm Estate. Cherry Garden Road was served by the 3 whilst the 7a passed through Old Town on route to Brodrick Road (Hampden Park). Services which worked via Ocklynge included the 10 from the railway station via Mill Road and 7 Devonshire Park - Brodrick Road. In 1965 services from the Marsden Farm Estate at Langney commenced running up to Ocklynge and by 1968 had incorporated the old Carew/Mill Road route No 10. Running over the new Lottbridge Drove was 14 linking Lindfield Road (Hampden Park) with Ocklynge, hourly.

After fifteen years of regular service No 16 (JK9114) joined the open top fleet late in the summer of 1961. Delivered new in 1946 it was one of a batch of six Leyland Titan PD1s of which five were converted to open top. These replaced the second generation of seafront buses with the withdrawal of the Leyland TD4/5s and AEC Regents reducing the available open top fleet from nine down to five. The withdrawal of the PD1s came in 1968, they had last seen service the previous summer and until partial conversion of a Leyland PD2 in 1973 the Corporation had no traditional open top vehicles for its seafront services. The PD1s were finished in a livery of broken white with blue trim, No 16 carried adverts for service 6 on both sides, the only amendment on the display during seven years being a fares increase which saw an hours ride go from 1/6 (7.5p) to 2/- (10p). There was little change to the regular seafront service which ran from the railway station, via Meads to the Foot of Beachy Head, and then down the seafront to the Archery and is seen in Picture No 16 waiting at Princes Park. The other seasonal route to Hampden Park was lost in the mid sixties (Route 8). A more basic Parades route was run in the evenings and Sundays off season as 6a.

In the background of Picture 73 can been seen the poles supporting the overhead for the Modern Electric Tramway which ran out onto the Crumbles. This miniature tramway gave a flavour of how travel might have been if the turn of the century scheme for a tramway link to Pevensey Bay and Bexhill had been pursued.

A really white scene in the early 1960s is seen in Picture 74 when No 60 (HJK160) battled its way through one of the blizzards which marked the decade. No 60 is probably working a "short" from Langney or the Archery and is heading up Seaside. From a batch of five delivered in 1961 it was ordered with quite different weather in mind. Fitted with a translucent roof panel and full drop upper deck windows, it was intended to supplement the PD1 open toppers entering service replacing the ageing fleet of pre-war Titan and Regent open toppers by now 25 years old. This batch of Regent Vs were finished in broken white with blue trim including lining out, which would last be used on the Atlanteans of 1972. This particular bus was one of those chosen for use on Town Tours and received platform doors in 1968. Another two batches of Regent Vs were to arrive in 1962 and 1963, note how the registrations at this time had the first number the same as their year of delivery. The Regent Vs were to form the largest number of vehicles delivered to a particular body and chassis design.

72. Eastbourne Corporation No54, an AEC Regent V 2D3RV of 1956, represented the first generation of buses without exposed radiators. These together with subsequent PD2s would in turn give way to the modern high capacity rear engined vehicles.

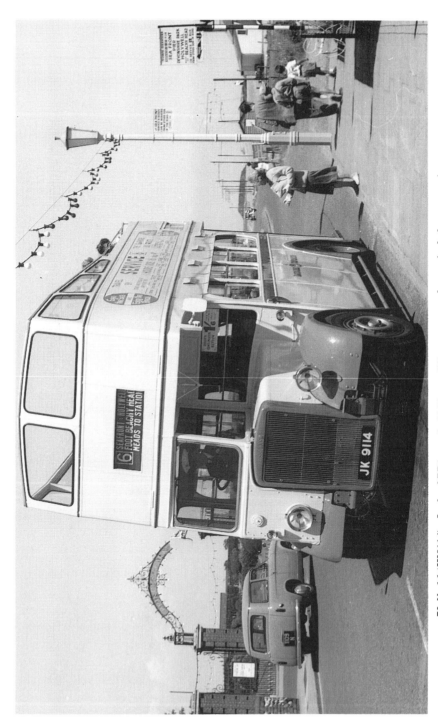

73. No 16 (JK9114) a Leyland PD1, new in 1946, gave fifteen years regular service before conversion to open top. It then spent another five years operating summer seafront services.

74. Regent V No 60 is at work in blizzard conditions in the mid 1960s. It was fitted with translucent roof panels and full drop windows, both with better weather in mind.

75. No 67 (KHC367) is seen working service 7a between Devonshire Park and Hampden Park in 1966. Before withdrawal and preservation it saw service on loan to London Country Bus Services.

76. Accidents were mercifully rare. However, after crashing into the Lamb Inn in Old Town No 66 was rebuilt by East Lancs. It was later converted into a recovery truck.

Delivered in 1963, No 67 (KHC367) is seen in Picture 75 in Old Town in around 1966. A decade later it would be found in less familiar surroundings whilst on hire to London Country Bus Services between February and June 1976.

Service 7a like most other Corporation routes in the 1960s continued through the decade without major changes, the other hourly service between Devonshire Park and Hampden Park being the 7 which worked via Ocklynge.

Although this last batch of Regent Vs had all been withdrawn by 1981, the famous radiator grill lived on with No 66 (KHC366) which was converted into a recovery vehicle, filling the gap left by the withdrawal of the Regent JK5603 (Monty) in 1965 which had left a Landrover as the sole recovery vehicle. No 66 had an unfortunate but thankfully rare accident in June 1965 when just two years old it crashed into the corner of the historic Lamb Inn at Old Town whilst working the Langney service 1/4 (see picture 76). By the end of the year the bus had been rebuilt by East Lancs (Neepsend) and returned to service.

There was a return to the Leyland fold in 1966 with the arrival of 10 East Lancs 60 seater Titan PD2a/30s which enabled the withdrawal of 1947/8 vintage Regent IIIs. Another batch of Leyland PD2s just over a year later proved to be the last traditional rear entrance vehicles bought new and the last delivered in the blue and yellow livery. A new era of vehicles was heralded in by Daimler Roadliners and Leyland Panthers in 1968. Like the Regent Vs and open toppers used on seafront duties, they were in a livery of overall broken white with a prussian blue band. In 1969 it was decided to adopt this as standard livery for all vehicles. Meanwhile the Titan PD2s carried the old livery well, the St Helens style grill being picked out in blue and the radiator filler cap carrying a badge. No 72 (BJK672) was of the first batch, again the registration (the first to bear a year suffix) denotes the year of delivery i.e. 672 = 1966. Also noticeable is the unusually high position of the registration plate and the introduction of two track route number blinds which were also being fitted to some Regent Vs. All the PD2 Titans survived into the 1980s.

In Picture 77, No 72 is leaving the Railway Station heading back down Terminus Road on its 14A hourly working which crossed Lottbridge Drove bound for the Hydneye.

Route development in the 1960s had seen the opening of services across Lottbridge Drove and services from Marsden Farm Estate, the only losses being seasonal open top runs on route 8 to Hampden Park.

Although the traditional front engined open platform double decker continued to provide the core of services throughout the 1970s, a new breed of vehicle was starting to make its mark. A new type of single deck bus was introduced starting in 1967 with the arrival of Leyland Panthers and Daimler Roadliners following. In 1968 Leyland Panther Cub No 92 (YTB771D) was purchased secondhand. It had been a demonstrator for Leyland and as such had been on loan to Eastbourne the previous September. Its Stachan bodywork was the odd one out, as all other single

77. No 72 (BJK672D) was a Leyland PD2a/30, new in 1966. The arrival of this batch enabled the withdrawal of Regent IIIs dating from 1947/8.

78. No 92 (YTB771D), its dual door arrangement intended to speed loading, was not a success in Eastbourne and the arrangement was not pursued on the new generation double deckers which followed. No 92 had already visited the town in September 1967 when working as a demonstrator.

79. Corporation bus passengers choke the pavement outside the railway station whilst in the foreground Southdown No 293 (HCD893) passes by on the hourly service 15 to Hastings, which was joint with Maidstone & District.

80. In January 1964 Pevensey Road bus station played host to Trent Motor Traction No 215 (215CCH), which was operating with Southdown in exchange for Southdown No 688.

81. Returning from its run to Birling Gap via East Dean, this Southdown Guy Arab II continued its open top seaside work until 1964 when it was displaced by PD3 "Queen Mary" types.

deck deliveries between 1967-71 carried East Lancs bodywork. This type of vehicle had been designed for one person operation; as elsewhere automated fare collection and staff reductions caused fury with the trade unions.

No 92 was built in 1966 and seated 43. Dual doors were intended to speed loading but this type of arrangement was not pursued on the new generation double deckers arriving in 1972. It would be an understatement to say that the Roadliners and Panthers were unreliable or unpopular for they were almost universally loathed; despite this No 92 served for 13 years. It was usually found on seafront and Meads services but in Picture 78 it is seen passing over the busy level crossing at Hampden Park on route 9. The importance of Hampden Park was increasing with the industrial estates along Lottbridge Drove and new residential estates at Hamlands and Winkney Farm. The new District General Hospital was constructed on Kings Drive.

Services carried on much as they had since the 1960s notable extensions being made to the new estates but it was the connection of Willingdon Drove with Lottbridge Drove which saw major changes with the provision of circular services in 1977. The increasing permutation of routes around Eastbourne serving new districts meant route number suffixes. For instance by 1980 route 4 had been supplemented by 4a, 4b, 4c, 4d, 4e and 4h at various times.

Residents of Hampden Park had been used to hourly services, a trend which became the norm on most Corporation routes throughout the town. With the complexity of routes passengers had increasing need of accessible timetable information. The small pocket sized folded timetable with route map used throughout the 1950-60s was replaced by a card covered booklet which without maps left much to be desired especially with the advent of circular services and ever diminishing blind displays. Luckily passengers on No 92 (YTB771D) had found their way on service 9 which provided a thirty minute frequency with journeys from either Brodrick Road or the Hydneye to Grand Parade or Devonshire Park.

Service 15 (operated jointly by Southdown and Maidstone & District) provided an hourly winter service uprated to twice an hour between July and September. It ran via Polegate, Hailsham, Hertmonceux, Ninfield and Bexhill to Hastings. Just as Southdown had opted for the all Leyland TD1 in the thirties, it again went for a Leyland product ordering 24 PD2s seen in Picture 79 of which No 293 (HCD893) was new in May 1947. In the background Corporation bus passengers congest the railway station frontage which offered sheltered but cramped conditions; even at Pevensey Road bus station facilities for Southdown passengers were lacking. Anywhere else perhaps in the British Isles, this Southdown bus would have seemed well groomed but the Corporation buses are its equal with their elegant hand painted advertisements. The livery on 293 represents the final standard which would last until NBC days.

January 1964 and the scene in Picture 80 at Pevensey Road bus station is a little different from usual with Trent Motor Traction Co No 215 (215CCH) about to set

82. The observer would not need Southdown PD3 No 284 to identify this as a Sussex scene, the flint walls being just one giveaway in this idyllic setting in the village of Jevington.

83. Southdown No 1945 (MCD45) had been displayed on the Duple stand at the 1952 Commercial Motor Shown.

off for East Grinstead on the 92. This vehicle was used for a month as part of an exchange in which Southdown No 688 (288AUF), a Marshall bodied single decker went north to Trent. Thus use of the 51 seat Willowbrook bodied Leyland PSU3/1R resulted in purchase of this combination for the Southdown fleet in 1968.

In May of 1964 Southdown also tried out 888DUK a Guy Arab V with Strachan bodywork which ran on routes 2 and 12. The 92 route to East Grinstead went via Hailsham, Nutley and Forest Row and took 2 hrs. 19 mins. Vehicles spent their layover period at the London Transport garage. This route had its origins in services 20/29 of the 1920s.

Maidstone & District had been allocated several batches of utility vehicles during the war. We have already seen how Southdown found the construction of these inferior and M & D lost no time in rebodying them. However Leyland PD2, Bristol K and their like were being replaced by the Leyland Atlantean rear engined double decker with the Maidstone Company being one of the first to standardise on them.

In less than perfect weather in Picture 81 No 426 (GUF126) has stopped outside Bradford's coal office on its return from Birling Gap via East Dean. This Guy Arab II new in 1944 had 56 seat Northern Counties bodywork which proved to be of more rugged construction than other utility bodies. In 1953 Southdown had rebuilt the body without front vents or side screen and in April 1959 they converted it to this distinctive open top style. It continued on seaside routes until 1964 when Leyland PD3 Queen Marys took its place.

Without the Southdown PD3 we would still recognise Picture 82 as a quintessential Sussex landscape with its characteristic flint stone walls and so many charming features that remind us of an English village. Note the vicar by the lane to St Andrews Church, the climbing rose and the tea rooms. Bus No 284 (BUF284C) like its many sister vehicles has attracted a devoted following over the years, they gained the affectionate nickname "Queen Marys" due to their length. No 284 was one of 38 similar vehicles delivered in 1965, four of these being capable of conversion to open top. Southdown remained loyal to the traditional design of bus albeit with full fronts. It was not until 1967 that the last of the type arrived.

Service 93 was acquired from Twines Services Limited in 1929 and services started from Langney Road running hourly alternately to Jevington and Wannock. During the war services were transferred to Pevensey Road bus station. Frequency was reduced later to two hourly and took 27 minutes for this pleasant rural ride.

Two very different designs of coach are seen passing the station in the early 1960s operating the South Coast Express in Picture 83. No 1645 (MCD45) entered the Southdown fleet in 1953 after having been exhibited on the Duple stand at the 1952 Commercial Motor Show. It was the only one of its batch to have a flush fitting door and only had a couple of years to go before withdrawal in 1965. Behind it, six years younger but with a Burlingham body design past its prime, is No 40 (VUF940), a

84. 1st November 1962; one of Southdowns services in the countryside around Eastbourne was the 98 which ran every three hours between Seaford and Hailsham.

Commer Avenger IV. 70 vehicles of this chassis type entered service between 1956 and 1962, this particular vehicle lasting until 1967.

Pioneer long distance routes started in the early days of the century but public confidence in this mode of travel was shattered by the infamous Handcross Hill accident which killed 10 passengers in 1906. Gradually a network of services radiating from the capital was established. Notable was the London Coastal Coaches central booking office at Victoria in whose network were operators such as Southdown. Although there had been journeys along portions of the coast it was the Royal Blue service in 1929 which sparked competition between Bournemouth and Margate, this eventually resolved itself when Royal Blue took over the Wilts and Dorset section of the service which was joint with Southdown and East Kent.

In Picture 84 we see a service which will not reach Eastbourne, yet it served many of the surrounding communities as Southdown route 98. It originated as the 27 which ran from Brighton Aquarium to Berwick (starting in January 1922) but by the mid twenties had been cut back to operate between Seaford and Berwick with about four return journeys a day. At weekends one journey was extended to Eastbourne via Polegate. Renumbered as service 26 in June 1928, its frequency was increased to run every other hour which remained unchanged right through to the end of the war. Peace brought about another change of number and route which was amended to 98 Seaford to Golden Cross, changed a couple of years later to Seaford - Hailsham which was the route as photographed at Exceat Farm on 1st November 1962. Starting from Seaford it crossed Exceat Bridge then passed through Littlington, Alfriston (where it reversed), Berwick, Upper Dicker, Horsebridge Mill and finally Hailsham High Street. The journey took 75 minutes and was three hourly daily. Extra journeys were provided between Seaford and Berwick station and between Upper Dicker and Hailsham. No 1506 (LUF506) was a Leyland with East Lancs single deck bus body seating 40 which was new in 1952.

Over the years the script fleetname used on saloons was gradually reduced to fill just one panel. In Picture 85 is a Leyland Leopard which has relatively stylish bodywork to a BET design built by Marshall. This was the standard single deck design introduced for one man operation and when new in 1967 seated 45. The Southdown livery does much to show off what was really quite a plain structure. The front was a particular feature of this batch typified here by No 173 (KCD173F) which is in Cornfield Road ready for the return journey to Seaford on service 126. This hourly working was typical of Southdown's network around Eastbourne which when incorporated into the NBC had changed little in the past decade. Benefits from the National Express network came by way of additional express journeys as far afield as Lancashire and Yorkshire.

A summary of Southdown services finds cross Downs services to Brighton running half hourly along the coast (12) or hourly inland via Lewes (25). Stage carriage connections northwards were via Uckfield (92) or Heathfield (95), whilst to the north east there were the 190-191-192 group which were part of the "Heathfield Pool" joint with Maidstone & District. Also joint with M & D to the east were the

Hastings routes 99 via the coast or 15 inland. Southdown still maintained the prized routes to Beachy Head worked as the 97 and 197 running according to season although frequencies were reducing. Local services were still provided to Jevington (93), Polegate (94), Pevensey - Pevensey Bay (96) or via the coast road (199). There was a twice weekly run to Hellingly Hospital and as already mentioned an extensive but mainly seasonal network of long distance routes plus Southdown's traditional high quality tours and regular programme of excursions.

The modern town of Hailsham can no longer boast a railway station or a bus garage and is almost expanding into a suburb of Eastbourne but for many years it was an unremarkable but typical Sussex market town through which ran the much lamented Cuckoo Line. The Southdown bus garage lay beyond the market. Along the coast Maidstone & District operated the Hastings Tramways trolleybus system which was fully absorbed into the M & D fleet in the late fifties. In 1958 replacement of electric traction commenced using Leyland Atlanteans such as No DL54 (54DKT) in Picture 86 which has arrived at Vicarage Fields, Hailsham whilst working the 15 joint service. The L in the fleet number denotes a lowbridge vehicle, built with Weymann bodywork on a PDR1/1 chassis. It was rebuilt to MkII specifications in 1963. It was withdrawn from the M & D fleet in 1975 and passed to Western National for further service within the National Bus Company.

85. Southdown No 173 (KCD173F) carries BET designed bodywork built by Marshalls and was typical of the single deck buses purchased for one person operation. Here it is on service 126 to Seaford.

86. Maidstone & District were amongst the first to purchase the Leyland Allantean with a batch being used for the replacement of the Hastings trolleybuses. DL54 (54DKT) was from amongst this batch and appears on the joint service 15 in Hailsham, the other operator being Southdown.

6. THE SEVENTIES - INNOVATION

To Stem Decline In Passengers.

Most of the Corporation fleet of Leyland Panthers which arrived between October 1970 and August 1971 were later destined to spend the majority of their revenue earning days along the coast at Bexhill, where they formed the basis of the Bexhill Bus Company. The batch was numbered 1-10 in the Eastbourne fleet (HHC901-10J), they were officially designated Leyland Panther PSUR1A/1R with East Lancs bodywork seating 43. The design was not one of Leylands best, numbers produced were limited, and despite this the maintenance staff managed to obtain reasonable serviceability.

Bus services had been relocated from the railway station into Terminus Road. Wishing to take advantage of the new road layout and the multi-storey carpark, a short lived "centre service" operated in the winter of 1978/9. Restrictions on car parking in the town centre together with pedestrianisation did little to stem the decline in bus passengers. Attempts to encourage wider use of buses included the introduction of a Travel Card which was publicised on all buses and could also be used on Southdown and Maidstone & District services within the Borough boundaries.

Route No 8 had previously been used to cover journeys to Hampden Park. It originated in the 1930s and later described seasonal open top services from Princes Park. When No 6 was photographed in Picture 87, Service 8 was being used on the Grand Parade - Hydneye service which ran from 1971 - 1975. It has since been used intermittently to cover routes between Meads and Cherry Gardens. On this occasion it was timetabled for Memorial Square and is about to commence its return journey, although the destination is unambiguous, route details are absent.

Picture 88 is yet another view taken outside the railway station, yet it provides a rare glimpse of No 94 (MJK94L) in service as it spent most of its life at the hands of the mechanics, on brief duties as a trainer and thereafter languishing in the yard at the Churchdale Road depot. No 94 was a Seddon Pennine IV seating 25 and was very much in vogue in the early 1970s. In Manchester large numbers provided inter station services and they even experimented with battery powered version. Eastbourne's intentions for their Seddon included replacement of the 1950 AEC Regal, taking over its contract duties and providing support for proposed minibus services to outlying estates. Route 3 was one of the few services on which No 94 performed regularly. By now this route commenced at Langney Point and ran to Cherry Gardens at Old Town, a journey whose origins lay back in the 1920s. On this occasion the working appears to terminate at the station.

Services to Old Town and Ocklynge continued much as they had been in the war with the backbone 1 still running every 12 minutes. Services 2/2a started from St

87. Limited numbers of Leyland Panthers were constructed. It was not one of Leylands best designs but Eastbourne's examples soldiered on and after withdrawal by Eastbourne spent many years with the Bexhill Bus Company. No 6 is seen in earlier days working Route 8, which provided a link between Grand Parade and the Hydneye at Hampden Park.

88. Seldom seen in service was Seddon Pennine No 94 (MJK94L) which had originally been intended to replace the AEC Regal on contract duties. This rare sighting caught it at work on Route 3 which ran between Langney Point and Cherry Garden Road, Old Town.

Philips Avenue whilst 7a/7 travelled to Hampden Park via Old Town and Ocklynge respectively. Carew Road services to Ocklynge were covered by 4a ex Tanbridge (Marsden Farm Estate) and the 4 ran every 15 minutes from either The Archery or Langney. In 1975 Langney services were extended to the new District Shopping Centre on selected workings but it was in 1977 with the introduction of 10a/c circular services that frequencies on the long standing 1/4 routes were reduced. Connections with Hampden Park had a new route to Old Town via Rodmill Drive, the Rodmill Estate had been one of the areas targeted for a dial a bus service on which No 94 was to have provided back up for the Ford minibuses.

The two Fords No 40/41 (OHC68M and XVX299L) were on loan from 1973 but were subsequently purchased by East Sussex County Council in 1975 following local government restructuring. Several residential developments such as Rodmill, Willingdon Park and Willingdon Trees were without bus services. Edward Leach who had taken up the position of Transport Manager in 1971 thought out a scheme to serve such estates. Intending passengers could book ahead by telephone for the bus to call at their home, also there would be hail and ride sections of the routes. These proposals were the first of many schemes since tried around the country, however routes still required licensing by regional traffic commissioners who eventually agreed to the Dial a Ride side of the operation only, which duly commenced on November 5th 1973. The concept proved to be ahead of its time and regular bus services eventually replaced some of the routes.

The Fords carried simplified fleetnames, logos for the Dial a Ride service and fleetnumbers but it was the Seddon No 94 which last carried the legend "Eastbourne Corporation" from new. Its broken white body had a wide central blue band and grille, which did little to relieve the angular body style. In future all new vehicles would carry the "EBC" logo (Eastbourne Borough Council) - the design of which was the work of a local student.

Leaving the pier No 15 (Picture 89) would run along Marine Parade passing down a slope which joined it with the higher Grand Parade. At this point coaches turn around the Royal Sussex Regiment memorial which was unveiled in 1906. Continuing toward Princes Park it would pass the area once known as Sea Houses, then the Redoubt Fortress and finally on the left the old Southdown garage now demolished. The continued appearance of Southdown PD3 "Queen Mary" open toppers and Bristol VRs rather eclipsed borough operations in this period but on 12th April 1978 the Transport Department was proud to celebrate its 75th anniversary with a convoy of buses retracing the original route of 1903, passengers being issued with special souvenir tickets. Most of the fleet carried advertisements to remind the townsfolk of their transport heritage.

Photo 89 shows the unfriendly greeting for visitors looking out for a ride along Eastbourne's renowned seafront esplanades. The "exact fare please" slogan was carried by the six Leyland Atlanteans delivered in 1972. No 15 (KHC815K), the fifth in the batch, was one of a new generation of rear engined double deckers seating 76 with front entrance for driver only operation. Sister vehicle No 16 gained fame

89. Woe betide the unwitting day tripper who fails to tender the correct fare for a ride on Atlantean No 15 (KHC815K). The year is 1974 and it has just received its new Eastbourne Borough Council logo.

90. Service 4a served the Marsden Farm Estate at Langney and ran to Ocklynge via Carew Road. The distinctive sounds of the engine of an AEC Regent V were becoming rarer by the time of the mid 1970s scene.

as the first in the fleet to carry all over advertisements, a gaudy display for a local travel company which it carried for over a decade; yet another source of revenue to offset increasing operating costs. The bodywork of Nos 11-16 by East Lancs had a more rounded finish than future batches but was almost identical to the Atlanteans purchased secondhand from Southampton City Transport in 1983.

As delivered the livery was broken white with a prussian blue band below lower deck windows and two thin blue lines above them. On this occasion it is seen opposite the pier on the 6a bound for Princes Park around 1974 having just received the EBC logo. Borough Council seafront services in the daytime were usually worked by open topper No 84; there were also Southdown services running to Beachy Head. In 1974 daytime route No 6 ran from the station to Meads, the Foot of Beachy Head and The Archery while the 6a provided a more limited service long the parades off peak. These services, which were amongst the earliest to run in Eastbourne, continued throughout the 1970s-80s with seasonal adjustments to their timetables. The routing of service 3 along part of the seafront provided services throughout the year. A breakthrough came in 1983 when scheduled services of the Borough transport finally reached the top of Beachy Head, although it was already passed on the extended Town Tour. Nominally this was route 16 for the first year, while the 6 ran to Meads from Langney Point.

Route 6 finally passed into history in 1984 when seafront services were renumbered in the 3... series. 6a was used again in the late 1980s to describe schools workings.

The Corporation's AEC Regent V fleet lost much of its sparkle when repainted in the lacklustre white livery. Picture 90 dates from the mid 1970s just before No 63 (JJK263) received its EBC logo; it only had a few years of active service to go before withdrawal in 1979. It had been new in 1962, part of the batch consisting of Nos 61-65 which formed the third order for AEC Regent Vs. Service 4a served the Marsden Farm Estate (Tanbridge Road) and went up to Ocklynge every hour via Carew Road. It was during this period that Langney services were revised to include what was originally known as West Langney, later including the Langney District Shopping Centre. Other services on the Langney - Ocklynge corridor saw no less than four departure points on service 4, two of which now started from Hampden Park. The various permutations in this series eventually reached 4H.

Towards the end of its career No 63 lost its AEC grill badge, a popular item amongst collectors. The municipal coat of arms was not lost when the EBC logos were applied but was reduced to a small representation of the side of the bonnet and on the rear. With their translucent roof panels giving a light airy top deck and their distinctive engine sounds they would be missed but in an age of one person operation they had become uneconomic to operate.

In Picture 91 there is an interesting line up at the Corporation Churchdale Road yard in early February 1981 with just one of the quartet of secondhand Leyland Atlanteans missing. Purchased from Ipswich Borough Transport in December 1980, No 63 (the vehicle missing from this view) had already been on loan in the

91. Three out of four secondhand Leyland Atlanteans purchased from Ipswich Borough Transport in December 1980 are seen together in Churchdale Road garage.

92. Winter services on Southdown Service 99 required only single deckers such as this Leyland Leopard which had been new in 1963, later converted for one person operation it is pictured passing the sewage pumping station at the Archery.

previous autumn running with the temporary fleet number 51. The batch was numbered 63-6 (LDX73-6G), they carried ECW bodywork and were originally delivered to Ipswich in 1968.

In the spring of 1985 No 65 & 66 were converted to open top, the first such complete rebuilds for over twenty years. After four years running in the standard fleet livery they were put into the paint shops and emerged resplendent as the "Eastbourne Queen" and "Eastbourne King", complete with gold lining out they carried red/biscuit and blue/biscuit livery respectively.

One Person Operation or OPO together with the application of National Bus Company logo firmly date the scene in Picture 92 in the early seventies, although the traditional Southdown livery still looks fresh on No 108 (108CUF), by now a decade old. A Leyland Leopard delivered with 51 seater Marshall bodywork at the end of 1963 it was converted for OMO in 1966 and downseated to 45. During the peak season working of the 99 would normally be by double deckers but during the winter the service only saw eight return trips a day. On this return journey from Hastings it is seen passing the sewage pumping station opposite the Archery. Much of the journey was over more pleasant landscape including Pevensey whose famous castle walls once enclosed the Roman town of Anderida. The hourly service 96 continued through Pevensey to Pevensey Bay (a village of far more recent origin) but its terminus at Beachlands was close to the hamlet of Normans Bay, notorious as the landing place of the invasion fleet in 1066.

On 14th March 1968 the BET group (to which Southdown belonged) sold its UK bus interest to the government, thus together with the already state owned Tilling group formed the National Bus Company. In Eastbourne this had little immediate effect, the first outward signs of the NBC became apparent throughout the Southdown operating area in September 1972 when a NBC corporate livery was introduced. Buses throughout the NBC would generally receive either an overall red or green livery. Southdown vehicles received the apple green option with the double N logo in white, the only relief being a broad white band. In the Eastbourne area the small dormy shed at Alfriston was closed and the town was to quickly see the results of standardisation on vehicles. Makes such as the Leyland National, Leyland Atlantean and Bristol VR quickly became the norm but in 1977 the most numerous vehicle type within the Southdown fleet remained the popular PD3. Eastbourne's allocation of vehicles included those housed at Crowborough, Hailsham and Uckfield together with those parked in the open at Seaford. They totalled 71 vehicles, made up of 25 single deck buses, 4 dual purpose single deckers, 24 coaches, 5 Leyland Atlantean double deckers plus just 8 Leyland PD3s. The open top contingent comprised 3 PD3s and 2 Bristols from the Brighton Hove and District fleet. The fleet was relatively modern with a majority of vehicles well under 10 years old and the year saw the arrival of an entire batch of 10 Leyland Nationals in Eastbourne.

93. Despite the special nature of seaside leisure services the splendid fleet of Southdown open top PD3s were subjected to the standard National Bus Company livery of apple green with a white band as seen on No 426 (BUF426C) working the 197 to Beachy Head.

94. Southdown fleet of Leyland PD3s were known by enthusiasts as "Queen Marys" because of their great length, although a little ponderous and difficult to drive they were popular and were used on the last crew operated services in the Eastbourne area, in this case service 94. The year is 1975.

95. Other than the double N logo, car No 414 (414DCD) has yet to be dressed in its new corporate NBC livery but the image to come is evident on the Bristol VR in the background.

96. Seen at the war memorial in full NBC livery heading out to Uckfield is car No 206 (KUF206F).

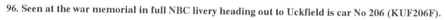

In Picture 93 No 426 (BUF426C) is travelling across the Downs on the by now familiar 197 to the Top of Beachy Head. It had been new in June 1965 and was one of the fleet of convertible open toppers purchased by Southdown, a practice which was perpetuated in NBC days with open top Bristol VRs. Despite their special place in the fleet aimed entirely at the tourist market, the open toppers received the standard livery. No 426 has a good load and judging from the open cab window and door the 7th July 1977 was a scorcher.

The first vehicle in the National Bus company to carry an all over advertisement was Southdown No 915 (6915CD); the background colour was red and promoted a chain of off licences. This livery was carried from December 1971 until April 1975, other PD3s carrying all over adverts and later promotional material for the company and regional events. In Picture 94, No 915 is passing Corporation PD2 No 77 and behind them is Panther No 4. A decade earlier the PD3 design offered a large capacity vehicle based upon solid traditional designs but when one man operation of double deckers was legalised in 1966, their days looked numbered. A bit ponderous and a little uncomfortable to drive they were, however, reliable. 915 was from a batch designated PD3/5 as opposed to PD3/4 and had an automatic clutch which resulted in problems starting off on hills. As routes over the Downs had several severe gradients they were earmarked for reallocation to the flatter parts of the operating area in the West but several lingered in Eastbourne. This batch also boasted fluorescent lighting and illuminated off side advertisement panel, as seen here.

As OPO spread the "Queen Mary" (PD3) was found less on stage duties and more often on contract schools and works journeys but service 94 was one the last conversions with crew operation lasting until April 1975. In this view 915 had left Stone Cross twenty six minutes earlier passing through Polegate and Willingdon village. The next bus in thirty minutes time would be on the Dittons Wood service a shorter route which alternated with the Stone Cross working.

The introduction of National Bus company livery to Southdown vehicles followed a pattern set out for component companies, the logo with its double N was applied with a rather bland fleetname over the current livery. Other than this in Picture 95 No 414 (414DCD) has yet to be subjected to corporate identity. Delivered in March 1964, it still retains a small script fleetname on the grill. In the background a Bristol VR stands as a reminder of things to come. It is in overall NBC green whilst waiting to work the 99 service to Hastings. Entrance to the cramped bus station was via Susans Road, a particularly sharp turn in for a PD3, and unwary pedestrians who had ignored the warning signs often fled before an advancing bus. Facilities increased little over the years and for a town of Eastbourne's stature did little for its image. One way traffic and pedestrian lights together with barriers along the pavement now guided those on foot who were faced with increased traffic speeds. The scene in Pevensey Road now bore little resemblance to the era when Southdown services had first penetrated the town fifty years earlier. Route 12 set off from the bus station at 7 minutes past the hour, heading for Pool Valley in Brighton.

97. Leyland Atlantean No 29 (VDY529T) was typical of the Eastbourne fleet intake in the late 1970s. It saw a decade of service in the town before passing into the joint Eastbourne/Southdown Hastings Topline operation in Hastings.

98. The Dennis Dominators such as No 40 (MPN140W) carried the usual East Lancs body available at the time. In this view No 40 is heading down Langney Rise.

Service 191 had been part of the Heathfield pool shared with Maidstone & District which provided a two hourly schedule between Eastbourne and Tunbridge Wells but by the late 1970s it was the preserve of Southdown and terminated at Uckfield. It ran every other hour alternating with the 192, the difference being in routing around Horsebridge and Hellingly. The 192 had previously been used to cover the Heathfield - Uckfield section of the route. Within Eastbourne route revisions had seen long familiar services replaced by the 95-96 group which included the 95A circular working. The areas affected included Polegate, Willingdon and Hailsham. Areas in the surrounding countryside not on regular bus routes benefitted from Royal Mail Post buses. Two such routes were operated by the Post Office and vehicles could be glimpsed in the PO yard. These services were Hailsham - Bodle Street Green and Heathfield - Waldron.

Seen at the war memorial in Picture 96, heading out for Uckfield, is No 206 (KUF206F) with Willowbrook body. It was already outdated by the Leyland National design which entered service in 1973 onwards and any attraction the Leopard may have had is now obliterated by the NBC livery. However for the visitor such refinements probably passed unnoticed and attractions along the route would include Michelham Priory, dating back to the 13th century and heavily restored. Hailsham deprived of its much lamented Cuckoo line by the Beeching axe was firmly within Southdown's network of Eastbournes operations. The days of Hailsham as a sleepy town of rope makers where the curfew sounded nightly at eight had long since passed.

No 29 (VDY529T) in Picture 97 was a Leyland Atlantean typical of Corporation fleet intakes between 1975-80. New in 1978, No 29 saw just a decade of service in Eastbourne before passing out of the regular fleet to the Hastings Topline operation in Hastings. Just two Atlanteans with East Lancs bodies remained by 1991.

The East Lancs body design remained on the Dennis Dominators such as No 40 (MPN140W) seen in Picture 98 passing down Langney Rise. Although deliveries of this type ceased in 1982 a further example did join the fleet in 1990 purchased secondhand from Brighton Borough Transport Limited. It was new to Tayside Regional Council in 1981.

Service 1a provided an hourly route between Shinewater and Filching Road, Old Town. The 1a was historically one of the first numbers used on Corporation services, being used after World War II to describe the St Philips Avenue to Old Town Service. Revisions in 1989 eliminated the 1a from the timetable after various guises.

7. ALL CHANGE FOR THE EIGHTIES

After purchasing Leyland Atlanteans from Ipswich, more secondhand acquisitions were made in 1983 with three Leyland Atlanteans from Southampton City Transport, these being similar to the original East Lancs bodied examples in the Eastbourne fleet. No 69 (TTR162H) lingered on in the fleet but after several periods out of service and it was finally sold to a dealer in the autumn of 1989. In Picture 99 No 69 had recently emerged from the paintshops and was working the 7, an hourly service as were most by 1983. No 67 and 68 were used for trials of new fleet liveries.

May 1985 and ex Ipswich Leyland Atlantean No 66 (LDX76G) (Picture 100) has an outing on service 3 after emerging from the workshops in its open top guise, complete with attractive illustrations of seafront features advertised by the Eastbourne Hotels Association. Livery is the new standard of biscuit and blue and, along with sister vehicle No 65, represented a return to traditional open top vehicles. Route 3 covered ground not formally served by open top vehicles as it fran from the Langney District Shopping Centre thence via Langney Point and the Pier to Terminus Road. The original Ramsay Way/Langney Point service running from 1972 to 84 served Osborne Road in Old Town.

During the summer of 1985 new options were tried for open top operations with the 3a running from Terminus Road to the Pier and up the seafront to the Top of Beachy Head, whilst the remaining PD2 in its restored "traditional" livery of blue and yellow operated the 3b from Langney to Beachy Head. Visitors could enjoy one of three daily coach operated town tours.

A return to the more usual pattern of open top services was seen in the following years but use of the open toppers was not restricted to special services, with peak hour requirements often calling for their use in the morning rush much to the enjoyment of children on their way to school on a warm summer day.

The Eastbourne Buses/Southdown joint venture in Hastings started operation in 1987 under the marketing name of Hastings Topline Buses. It utilised a variety of vehicles sourced from both Companies although the basis was Leyland Nationals from Southdown and Leyland Atlanteans from Eastbourne. The reality of every day service requirements and maintenance requirements meant that most types of Eastbourne vehicles, including their dual-purpose coaches, ran on Hastings Topline routes, especially the 98/99 Eastbourne - Hastings service. In Picture 101, No 32 (YJK532V), still owned by Eastbourne Buses, is setting out on the coastal run to Hastings in May 1987. New in August 1979, it was one of a batch of eight Atlantean AN68s with 82 seat East Lancs bodies. The Hastings Topline fleetname, black on yellow, had been applied on the non standard all cream livery which was a remnant of the colour scheme trials.

99. Secondhand double deckers continued to arrive in the Eastbourne Buses fleet; in this case originating from Southampton City Transport were Leyland Atlanteans. No 69 (TTR162) is resplendent in its fleet livery, having first appeared in the colour of the former operator.

100. Ex Ipswich Atlantean No 66 (LDX76G), one of the duo of open toppers, is seen with paintings depicting scenes along the seafront. This artwork was sponsored by the Eastbourne Hotels Association.

101. The Hastings Topline venture in Hastings originally utilized Atlanteans from Eastbourne and Leyland Nationals from Southdown. Here No 32 (YJK532V) is still owned by Eastbourne Buses.

102. Not what is seems, this apparent intruder from Southdowns West Sussex division is really Eastbourne No 140. By this time passengers were getting used to variations in operators and liveries in the aftermath of deregulation.

On 29th May 1988 a separate Company was formed named Wainfleet Ltd which became Hastings Topline Buses Ltd. With the formation of the new Company No 415 (YJK532V) was selected as the candidate for preparation in the new yellow and black livery which emerged from the paintshop in April 1988. It was also the first bus in the fleet to carry full size Hastings Topline fleetnames. One feature which did not survive was the Hastings Topline operation of route 99 which passed back to Eastbourne Buses control.

Picture 102 shows not a long distance service to Eastbourne from Southdown's West Sussex division but Eastbourne No 140 (OKJ507M). As can been seen it has arrived from the Southdown fleet carrying one of the divisional liveries which involved a dark green skirt to pseudo traditional livery. Although the sticker in the windscreen states that the vehicle is on hire, it had on paper at least been sold in May, the previous month. It was delivered new in 1973 to Maidstone & District and passed to Southdown in 1981. Later renumbered 13 in the Eastbourne fleet it was eventually displaced by shorter Leyland Nationals purchased secondhand and was sold on to Brighton Buses in 1989. By 1987 bus services in the provinces were fully deregulated, a process which had begun with the 1985 Transport Act, culminating in "D" Day on 26th October 1986. This followed a year when operators had registered their commercial services and were restricted as to changes and curtailments of services. Where operators had failed to register services the county councils identified routes which were socially desirable and tenders invited on the basis of awards to those requiring least subsidy. Such services in East Sussex would be referred to as "Local Riders" services. These contracts, often for short periods, led to changes in operators which confounded the already baffled travelling public faced with a stream of changing liveries in the area.

Eastbourne purchased route 201 from Vernons Coaches in 1986. The route was very rural running via Hailsham and Cowbeech to Rushlake Green and gave the erstwhile municipal operator its first country route which was joined by a twice weekly Jevington service. The 201 route included journeys to Heathfield and short workings to Hailsham in 1987; it was extended back through to Eastbourne rather than starting at Langney and renumbered 214.

The Hastings Topline venture in Hastings was partly made possible by tendered school workings in that town. Other out of town routes were gained between Uckfield and East Grinstead in February 1988. Commercial services now extend to destinations in the heart of rural Sussex such as Battle and even seasonal routes to New Romney.

The Rushlake Green service continued and by 1991 included four journeys to Uckfield. Double deck workings were not unknown and what better vantage point is there than the upper deck of a British Bus despite possible threats from the EC to eliminate such designs.

103. This PD3/11 was received from Blackpool in exchange for opentop No 84.

104. Wadham Stringer bodied Leyland Swift F956XCK was allocated a temporary fleet number of 603 when it worked with Eastbourne Buses as a demonstrator in May 1989.

Eastbourne Buses Ltd have provided several unusual acquisitions in recent years, not the least being the exchange in 1989 of PD2A/30 open topper No 84 (DHC784E) for Blackpool Transport Services Limited PD3/11 (LFR532F), which received the current Eastbourne fleet livery. The February 1990 view (Picture 103) shows it working the 20, which at the time was an hourly service between Langney and Hill Road. Numbered 81 in the fleet, the bus carries 71 seater MCW bodywork.

By May 1990 service 20 had been cut back to Churchdale Road and by 1991 had given way to a new route 2 running from Terminus Road via Bridgemere Road to Langney. Rationalisation of the fleet enabled fewer spares to be held.There have been further purchases of secondhand vehicles, although a lot of new single deckers have arrived. Services out to country areas have remained a feature of the timetable whilst in the town three circular routes together with service 1 provided the backbone of services, following a major re-cast of services in 1989. Having secured a more sound financial status and operations on a scale within its abilities, it seemed likely that Eastbourne would retain a municipally owned bus company until government legislation changes the situation.

Allocated the temporary fleet number 603 (F956XCK) the vehicle in Picture 104 was a Leyland Swift demonstrator carrying Wadham Stringer "Vanguard" bodywork which seated 39. It was finished in a livery of deep cream with a red band and was used for a fortnight in May 1989 appearing mainly on services 8/8c. Both these hourly routes covering the Cherry Gardens - Meads areas derived from the Red Carpet service of 1986 and from the Meads - Cherry Garden route of 1984.

Demonstration buses had visited the municipal operator on many occasions over the years although following the early Clarkson Steam bus trails it was not until the 1950s that Leyland and AEC put their products on test in the town. Not quick to change from traditional products, vehicles tried out did not always results in orders but Strachan bodied Leyland Panther YTB771 did find a home in the fleet after its loan in 1967.

Developments in the UK bus industry in the mid 1980s were profoundly influenced by government policy towards nationalised industries. Already several had been sold off in the process now known as privatisation. This philosophy which was to extend to the National Bus Company was based upon the requirement to make and sustain profits. Unfortunately providing a comprehensive bus service or any other form of public transport is not always a reliable source of income; nevertheless a train of action was set in hand and events within Southdown were soon noticeable in the Eastbourne area.

1985 saw the 70th anniversary of Southdown Motor Services Limited; it was also the last year in production for the Leyland National but more striking to the eye were the results of divisional changes. At the beginning of 1985 the Company was divided

105. 1985 saw the split of Southdown into regional divisions, operations in the Eastbourne area coming under the East & Mid Sussex Sector. Car No 553 (NCD553M) carried the appropriate livery towards the end of the NBC era.

106. Southdown Leyland National No 68 (WYJ168S) is working a tendered service in Eastbourne and carries the post NBC livery which harked back to the traditional company colours, which are reputed to have been designed to reflect the colour of the South Downs.

into six, the Eastbourne operating area being in the "East and Mid Sussex" division. Although it had been decided at this stage not to set up separate Companies, the extensive reorganisation was implemented on March 1st and was intended to be more responsive to local requirements. Quickly the local division set about painting a double decker in a livery akin to the traditional green but with white instead of cream.

A new local timetable was introduced covering all services in Eastbourne, Hailsham and Seaford, this booklet giving the divisional manager's address as Cavendish Place in Eastbourne. By August the division was busy reinforcing its individual identity with vehicles repainted locally into a more proximate version of the old livery and, by the end of the summer, reference to the NBC and the use of its logos on publicity had all but vanished.

The NBC logo made its last appearance after special versions for the 70th anniversary and the Chairmans awards had been used. By the autumn it had been decided that Southdown, its engineering functions and Brighton Hove & District should be formally split into separate Companies as from 1st January 1986. By the end of 1985 several vehicles had appeared in the new livery amongst which was No 553 (Picture 105), the second double decker to be so treated.

No 553 (NCD553M) is a Bristol VRT SL6LX new in 1973 and had spent much of its life at Brighton but now in Eastbourne is working the 7 mile journey to Jevington via Polegate which took about 27 minutes.

Southdown No 68 (WYJ168S) had recently been transferred in from the Portsmouth area when photographed (Picture 106) on 16th May 1989. It had been repainted and received brackets for the small slipboard on the front panel. Southdown's workings were from Bridgemere to Terminus Road during the day and extended to Hill Road in the evenings. Alternative displays were available either side of the slipboard. The Leyland National which had been developed as a joint venture between the manufacturer and the National Bus Company remained the basis for single deck vehicles operations into Stagecoach days. In 1989 an extensive revision of Eastbourne Buses services was introduced and a new "network" commenced operation.

By the end of 1989 a new livery was becoming a familiar sight along the South coast as the first vehicles of the Stagecoach group emerged in corporate colours of overall white with blue, red and tan stripes. First were the vehicles of Southdown, then Cedarbus of Worthing, Portsmouth Citybus, Hastings Topline and finally Hastings and District. Although government intervention has since forced the group to sell off some Portsmouth operations, it was a remarkable tally of operators to be absorbed in so short a time. With its original base around Perth in Scotland the Stagecoach group soon established bases all over Britain. Just as Stagecoach had taken advantage of the 1980 deregulation of coach services, it was quick to take advantage of further legislative changes in 1986 to expand operations. The sell off of the National Bus Company allowed for the purchase of up to four Companies,

107. Although not the first minibuses to work in Eastbourne, the Hastings & District venture in Eastbourne did provide an Indian summer for passengers with several roads served for the first time.

108. The Lewes Coaches division of Brighton Buses is represented by No 81 (UTD203T) which was purchased secondhand from Southend Transport.

109. Although by no means typical of buses seen in Terminus Road, the transport enthusiast has an appetite for the unusual which is well catered for with this ex East Kent Regent V (PFN882).

110. Secondhand buses continued to be purchased and into the Eastbourne Buses fleet came the likes of this ex Colchester Borough Transport Leyland Atlantean which carried ECW bodywork.

the Stagecoach group accumulating Hampshire Bus and Pilgrim Coaches, Cumberland Motor Services and United Counties. Subsequent purchases of Companies which had bought NBC subsidiaries brought East Midland and Ribble into the fold plus the operations of the former Barrow municipal fleet. In August 1989 came Southdown and later Hastings & District.

The theory behind minibuses was that they were cheaper to purchase and operate and could run over roads unsuitable for "big" buses. Eastbourne had already seen the Southdown minibuses operating to Polegate via Willingdon and the corporation Red Carpet services plus of course the original Dial a Ride experiment. Derided by many as glorified bread delivery vans, Mercedes such as D952UDY No 852 in the Hastings & District fleet (Picture 107) was one of many purchased for their Hastings town services.

When Eastbourne Buses and Southdown started the Hastings Topline operation in Hastings it had broken the previous working arrangement which went back (with Maidstone & District) to 1920 whereby Southdown (and M & D on joint services) had protection by the 1930 Act.. The activities of Eastbourne Buses and Southdown in Hastings led to constant rumours of retaliation by the Hastings Company and when they finally started under the banner of "Eastbourne and District" the local press came out with headlines such as "bus war in Eastbourne".

The Hastings & District service under its local operating name provided a 10 minute frequency from Terminus Road to Shinewater at Langney and served some roads which had never seen a bus. The service numbered 19a started on 13th March 1989 and for the first week passengers travelled free of charge. Eastbourne Buses put on additional buses in Eastbourne. However, the Hastings operation was putting a strain on Eastbourne Buses which was already having difficulty in maintaining its scheduled services in the home town.

The Stagecoach group completed their domination of the East Sussex bus scene with the purchase of the Hasting & District buses, thus by the end of 1989 they had the Hastings & District, Hastings Topline and Eastbourne & District service, many of which were competing with their other acquisition namely Southdown. It was clear that a rationalisation of services would not be long in coming. Meanwhile No 852 speeds towards the Langney District Shopping Centre and Shinewater residents enjoy an excellent service.

One of the new names to appear on buses around Eastbourne after deregulation was Lewes Coaches. This division of Brighton Buses was formed from the small independent operator in Lewes which was purchased with buildings and vehicles in May 1988. Like Eastbourne Buses, out of town operations helped the Company achieve revenue urgently required as, although municipally owned, they were now Limited Companies charged with trading profitably. Economies pursued saw the influx of secondhand vehicles into fleets, in the case of Picture 108 an ex Southend Transport Leyland Leopard No 81 (UTD203T), now painted in the duo-tone blue and white of Lewes Coaches.

111. Competition resulted in Stagecoach vehicles appearing in a new livery. In this case No 623 (UWV623S) carries the mainly blue highly non standard livery together with the local marketing name "Eastbourne & District".

The joint Brighton Hove & District/Brighton venture with express services to Eastbourne started in May 1988 with connections at Eastbourne on the Hastings Topline derived route to Hastings. Weekday workings finished in Terminus Road but on Sundays routing was via the pier. By July 1988 Eastbourne Buses had taken over some former BH & D journeys on the X99 Brighton - Eastbourne section and by the winter BH & D involvement had ceased. Evening and Sunday services ended and weekday schedules reduced followed by the withdrawal of Eastbourne from the operation which left it an all Brighton affair, worked by their depots in Lewes and Brighton itself. In May 1989 all journeys were worked by Lewes Coaches with an increase in journeys again and some extensions through to Hastings.

Ex East Kent Regent V PFN882 in Picture 109 was probably the first independently owned double deck bus to operate in Eastbourne for sixty years it had passed from the Cavendish Coach Company to Vernons (Day and Butlands) still in its former operators livery of maroon and cream. The rural route into the Sussex heartland was to survive the eventual demise of Vernons in 1986 and was purchased by Eastbourne Buses. Originally based at Polegate, the Vernons operating centre became established at Westham, using a variety of secondhand single deck vehicles. Their stage carriage work became a byword for old fashioned courtesy and reliability. Using regular drivers, passengers identified with staff which promoted loyalty. Although this view of a double decker is not typical of Vernons vehicles, it represents the variety of types seen on Eastbourne's roads, often only for a brief period and not always captured on film.

Eastbourne Buses No 29 (NNO62P) in Picture 110 is one of an increasing number of ECW bodied vehicles purchased since 1990; in this case it was new to Colchester Borough Transport Limited in 1976 and arrived in Eastbourne at the beginning of 1991. Although outwardly similar to the vehicles purchased from East Kent, the Colchester examples had different interior layouts with forward ascending staircases rather than the NBC standard, ascending to the rear. The ECW Atlanteans replaced former London Transport dual door Leyland Nationals. Other sources of secondhand vehicles have been Greater Manchester Buses and London Country via various dealers.

112. Leyland Olympian No 57 (E857DPN) represents the largest batch of similar buses in the Eastbourne fleet in the 1990s; delivered in 1988 they were to later have their roofs painted blue to reduce painting costs.

The Eastbourne Omnibus Society

This society offers a warm welcome to anyone with an interest in buses. Monthly meetings are held and a regular newsheet contains news of local operators, together with articles by members covering operations far and near.

Contact Mr. J. Bishop, 48 Bramble Drive, Hailsham, East Sussex BN27 3HA.

8. SOME THINGS NEVER CHANGE

1993 marks the 90th anniversary of municipal bus operation in Eastbourne. The perilous nature of providing a profitable service in the 1990s was illustrated by the collapse of Maidstone Boroline in 1992. Eastbourne remains one of thirty five council owned bus companies in Britain with government policy still declared to be in favour of the total privatisation of ownership. The upheavals of the Eastbourne bus scene in the aftermath of deregulation have gradually faded away. The rogue card remaining is the seemingly constant reshuffle of county council tendered services.

The first change in livery came when the Leyland Olympians of 1988 vintage had their roofs painted blue as with No 57 (E857DPN) in photo 112. This batch with their Northern Counties bodywork broke the long tradition of East Lancs supplied bodies. Following the departure of most Atlanteans to the Hastings Topline operation, the Olympians were left forming the largest batch in the fleet.

There was happy news in 1991; it was the first year of the Eastbourne Omnibus Society's rally. Based in a field beside Drusillas Zoo Park at Alfriston it enjoyed glorious weather and visitors could participate by joining free bus services to Lewes bus station. The "Busmans Holiday" was deemed a success by all involved and was set to become a regular part of the season for Eastbourne's bus enthusiasts.

After a period of purchasing secondhand Leyland Atlanteans, Eastbourne Buses once again changed its vehicle policy and began a steady intake of new single deck buses following on from the first Dennis Javelins. Typical intakes were Dennis Darts with 35 or 43 seat bodywork to the Wadham Stringer Portsdown design, together with the larger Javelin with Wadham Stringer Vanguard II bodies seating 55. Unique was Dennis Javelin No 27 (J127LHC) which was furnished with "Derwent" bus bodywork supplied by Plaxton. This was used for the lengthy rural routes and was new to the Eastbourne fleet in July 1991. The following year it received a new livery as seen in photo No 113 seen waiting to set off on service 28. This route had started in 1990 serving Battle, Northiam and Rye on the way to Dungeness. Although only operated in July and August, the route was to become a regular service to Rye on weekdays. The number 28 was also used to cover workings on the former County Council tendered route between Bexhill and Sedlecombe. Much has been made of the leisure aspect of Eastbourne Buses routes in East Sussex, the Sunday version of the 28 is service 27 which is extended to New Romney where passengers have about four hours to explore the Romney Marshes and travel on the Romney, Hythe and Dymchurch Railway. The 28 also serves the Kent & East Sussex Railway at their Northiam Station. These and other services are heavily promoted through both the local information offices and the new Bus Stop Shop opened in the Arndale Shopping Centre in 1992, which replaced the bus kiosk in Terminus Road.

Despite the disposal of several of the secondhand Leyland Atlanteans, No 33 (JJG6P) remained active until 1992 and this former East Kent Road Car Company bus received promotional material for a playbus project. In connection with this

113. The Plaxton Derwent body on Dennis Javelin No 27 (J127LHC) was intended for dual purpose use.

114. The Alexander bodied Leyland Olympian was the new standard double decker for the Stagecoach group in 1991.

scheme No 33 appeared in the pedestrian precinct in July 1992 (see photo 114) and was accompanied by clowns and suitably festive high jinks. It was one of four ex East Kent vehicles which were joined by another two ECW bodied Atlanteans from Colchester Borough Transport Limited. Other interesting acquisitions in the 90s included a Bristol LHS6L; unpopular with drivers it lasted less than a year with Eastbourne Buses. From Brighton Buses came Dennis Dominator No 59 (JSL280X), new to Tayside in 1981 it passed to Brighton in 1985. Meanwhile the fleet of elderly Leyland Nationals had dwindled to just one pair of ex-London Country examples until withdrawal in 1992.

The provision of bus services by Eastbourne Buses around the town continued without dramatic change in the 1990s. The three-yearly competition for East Sussex County Council tendered routes also provides the impetus for unusual workings.

The year 1992 was another year of re-organisation within the Stagecoach Group with its South Eastern operations being grouped into three Companies. To the West is Stagecoach South Ltd trading as Hampshire Bus and Sussex Coastline Buses trading as Coastline. The area in which Eastbourne operations are allocated was named South Coast Buses, thankfully the name Southdown was retained for trading as was Hastings Buses. Legal lettering for the new Companies was quickly applied. The Stagecoach Group through the power of bulk purchasing became one of the most important customers for British bus output. The company chose two basic models for ordinary stage carriage work these being the Alexander bodied Leyland Olympian (photo 115) and the Dennis Dart also bodied in Scotland by Alexander. Car No 221 (J721GAP) is pictured working service 18 to Polegate, formally route 16/17 worked by minibuses, whilst Dennis Dart No 521 (J521GCD) is employed on local service 8 to Meads, the only jointly worked service (photo 116).

The Eastbourne Bus story has come a long way since the first tentative steps at mechanisation at the turn of the century. The hardships of the crews on the early horse omnibuses are long forgotten. However there are many people who have an interest in the continuing evolution of transport in Eastbourne and two societies exist to cater for such interest, details of the Eastbourne Omnibus Society and the Southdown Enthusiasts Club are given at the end of this book. In 1992 the Eastbourne Omnibus Society held its 2nd rally at Drusillas Zoo Park and offered a free bus service to Polegate railway station. In photo 117 we can see one of the oldest vehicle in the Eastbourne Buses fleet taking part in the fun. No 82 (DHC782E) dates from 1967 and is a Leyland Titan PD2A/30, this traditional front engined rear entrance vehicle requires crew operation, something of a rarity in the 1990s. This reminds us of those who work with buses in Eastbourne, although the hours are shorter, the responsibilities are just as great. The high capacity double decker working in crowded roads with fare collection, cards to check, foreign visitors to guide, to mention but a few tasks, is an onerous job. No less vital are those who provide the back up, in the sphere of maintenance and painting. The requirement to work towards a profit has seen the introduction of outside contracts, MOT work, vehicle parking and fuelling.

The future of buses in Eastbourne may not be that radical; we have already seen a return to full size vehicles after a storm of minibuses. Whatever the future holds it will be built upon the traditions of a town which can still boast two of the countries best known and respected operators and we look forward to the expansion and improvement of services into the 21st century.

115. Working jointly-operated local service 8 is the standard Stagecoach single deck vehicle, in this case the first Dennis Dart "Dash" allocated to Eastbourne.

116. Traditional vehicles can still be seen in Eastbourne; here No 82 (DHC782E) operates to Polegate on a special free service in July 1992.

117. Seen prior to delivery in 1992, this Wadham Stringer bodied Dennis Lance was registered to include the figure 90 to mark the impending anniversary. The fleet number is 13.

BIBLIOGRAPHY

Monthly newsheets of the Southdown Enthusiasts Club.
Monthly newsheets of the Eastbourne Omnibus Society.
"Buses and Trolleybuses before 1919" David Kay, Blandford Press 1972.
"History of British Bus Services, South East England" Colin Morris, Transport Publishing Company 1980.
"Eastbourne in Old Photographs", Cecile Woodford, Alan Sutton 1989.
"Short History of Eastbourne", Lawrence Stevens, Eastbourne Local History Group 1987.
Ward Locke Guides to Eastbourne. Various dates.
"Eastbourne Volume 1. A Portrait in Old Picture Postcards", John Wilton and John Smith, SB Publications 1990.
"Some Street Names of Eastbourne", Eastbourne Local History Group 1973.
"83 Years of Municipal Passenger Transport in Eastbourne", Eastbourne Buses Limited 1986.
"The Book of Eastbourne", W.G.Willoughby, GMC 1931.
"The Horse Buses of Brighton and Hove", Adrian Peasgood, Falmer Centre for Continuing Education 1985.
"Fleet History" 2PK5, PSV Circle Publication.
"Eastbourne Corporation Transport Department 1903-1963", E.B.T.D. 1963.
"Wartime Eastbourne", George Humphrey, Beckett Features 1989.
"The Motor Bus Services of Kent and East Sussex", Eric Baldock, Meresborough Books 1985.
"The Maidstone & District Illustrated Fleet History 1911-1977", The Maidstone & District and East Kent Bus Club 1977.
"The Southdown PD3s", Julian Osborne, Capital Transport 1985.
"Southdown", Colin Morris, Transport Publishing Company 1985.
"Southdown Fleetlist", Southdown Enthusiasts Club 1954 onwards.
"Southdown Review", Southdown Enthusiasts Club 1984 onwards.
"Southdown Route Working", Southdown Enthusiasts Club 1977.
"Interesting Independents, The South and East Anglia", Capital Transport, Gordon Watts 1988.
"Eastbourne Borough Motor Buses, The First 80 Years", Southdown Enthusiasts Club 1983.
"Eastbourne Historic Street Furniture", Eastbourne Local History Group 1984.
"Eastbourne Chronicle", various dates.
"Eastbourne Gazette", various dates.
"Eastbourne Herald", various dates.
"Eastbourne Directory", Gowlands 1877-1925.
Directory of Eastbourne, Kellys 1926 onwards.
"Eastbourne Blue Book and Directory", Pikes 1885 onwards.

PHOTOGRAPHIC CREDITS

Photograph Number

9,10,26,27,32,35,47,76.	Eastbourne Buses Limited
15,38.	J. Cooper
16,17,86.	Southdown Enthusiasts Club
19,22.	J. Maynard
30,48,57.	C.F. Clapper
31.	D.W.K. Jones
39.	S.L. Pool
49,51,56.	W.J. Haynes
53,54,58,61,62,64,75,81,82.	R.F. Mack
65,66.	E. Surfleet
67,73,77.	P.J. Relf
68,69,70,72,84.	C.W. Routh
74,78,87.	R. Simmons
80.	C.B. Wilkin
83.	D.D. Kirk
97,93,99,102,104,106.	P.R. Gainsbury
100,101,105,110,111.	E.C. Churchill
103,107.	A.P. Gainsbury
109.	Maidstone & Dist.Bus Club
117.	Wadham Stringer
Cover photographs	R.F. Mack

All other photographs by author or from his collection.

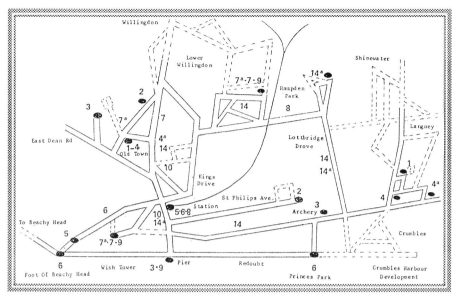

Eastbourne Corporation Bus routes - Summer 1965 with service numbers and termini. The completion of Lottbridge Drove provided alternative routes to Hampden Park but more importantly laid the foundations for the circular services which were to follow. The routes shown in outline are those additional areas served by Eastbourne Buses and Southdown in 1991, the main areas of the extension being the Langney, Shinewater, Willingdon and Lanney Point estates. Considerable changes have occurred in the detailed routing of buses particularly in the town centre and to Meads. This map should only be taken as a guide to areas served.

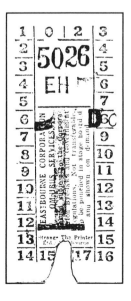
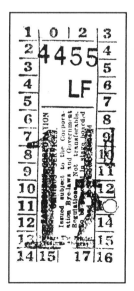
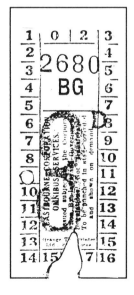